Paper
FLOWERS

Paper FLOWERS

35 beautiful step-by-step projects

Denise Brown

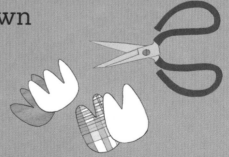

CICO BOOKS

LONDON NEW YORK

Published in 2014 by CICO Books
an imprint of Ryland Peters & Small
519 Broadway, 5th Floor, New York NY 10012
20–21 Jockey's Fields, London WC1R 4BW

www.rylandpeters.com

10 9 8 7 6 5 4 3 2 1

Text copyright © Denise Brown 2014
Design and photography copyright © CICO Books 2014

A CIP catalog record for this book is available from the
Library of Congress and the British Library.

ISBN: 978 1 78249 149 1

Printed in China

Editor: Marie Clayton
Design: Geoff Borin
Illustrations: Qian Wu
Photography: Jo Henderson
Stylist: Nel Haynes

CONTENTS

Introduction 6

Chapter 1

SIMPLE YET STUNNING

SPIRAL *Ranunculus* 10

SPRAY OF *Catkins* 13

GRAPHIC *Tulips* 16

LOOPY *Flowers* 18

CHRYSANTHEMUMS 21

SEED *Packets* 24

ORIENTAL *Poppies* 26

FRILLY *Fancies* 28

DAISY *Chains* 32

FALLING LEAF *Pompoms* 35

Chapter 3
SOPHISTICATED STYLE

FADED *Roses* 84

DANDELION *Clocks* 87

PEONY *Wreath* 90

THISTLE *Heads* 94

DOGTOOTH *Violets* 98

ELEGANT *Lilies* 100

MUSICAL *Roses* 103

VALENTINE *Flower* 106

CLIMBING *Vine* 110

HONESTY *Seedheads* 112

CHERRY *Blossom* 115

EXOTIC *Orchids* 118

Templates 120
Index and Acknowledgments 128

Chapter 2
BRIGHT AND BEAUTIFUL

ANEMONES 40

CUPCAKE *Poppies* 43

FLOWERING *Cactus Lights* 46

LOLLIPOP *Flowers* 50

WATERLILIES 53

TRIPLE *Pinks* 56

TOPIARY *Cones* 60

GRAPE *Hyacinths* 62

ORIGAMI *Flowers* 65

VIBRANT *Dahlias* 68

COLORFUL *Gerbera* 72

PATTERNED *Daffodils* 75

FIERY *Sunflower* 78

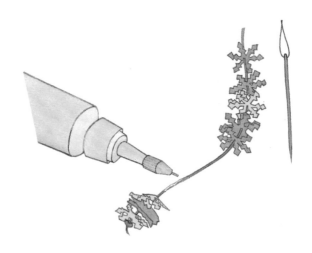

INTRODUCTION

I have wanted to do a book on paper flowers for a long time so was thrilled to work on this one. Despite my love of flowers I am no gardener—I use flowers for inspiration and don't try to replicate them. You won't find correct plant terminology in my projects—I refer to "yellow frill" or "flower base," because I think it makes instructions easier to follow. I love playing with scale and there's lots of scope for artistic license.

The paper is important; it has to have the right sort of "bend"—not too stiff so it cracks or too weak so it flops. Look for paper with color on both sides, such as double-sided giftwrap or copier paper, which comes in many colors. And catalogs look amazing transformed into flowers. I recycle junk mail for practice pieces, cereal boxes are excellent for templates, and I experiment with paper serviettes, kitchen roll, coffee filter papers, envelopes... Rainbow color tissue paper is one of my favorite mediums, even though it doesn't stretch. Crepe paper comes in various weights and stretchiness and with this you can mold petals, which I paint in watercolor for interesting effects. If you do paint or use chalks then fix the color—but try a test piece first to make sure the fixative doesn't splatter

and ruin your project. Ease crepe a little at a time because once it's stretched you can never go back—and grain direction is important, so check the grain line on the templates.

My favorite pieces of equipment are a scalpel, metal ruler, cutting mat, and fine nozzle glue dispenser. I don't use specialist equipment—I prefer a rustic, handcrafted look—but if time is an issue it can be great. I use 20 or 22 gauge wire, which is bendy. With glue, for large areas use spray glue; for hand-size areas try glue stick; for anything smaller, use white glue (PVA). Always allow to dry fully between stages.

I like to make leaves separately—there's no point in spending time on them only to find they are hidden in your favorite container. If your vase is opaque, fill it with dried rice—it holds the blooms firmly, yet you can move them around easily. In general, I try to avoid leaving flowers in direct sunlight.

I hope you enjoy making the flowers in this book—and that it will inspire you to come up with your own variations. Use scrap paper to practice first, and don't get frustrated if your first attempts aren't perfect—you will improve with practice!

Chapter 1
SIMPLE YET STUNNING

SPIRAL
Ranunculus

These spiral flowers are very easy to make and remind me of ranunculus; try them in different sizes and experiment with your own spiral designs. They look better in solid color paper because you can see the structure more easily, but make sure the paper you choose will bend properly.

1 Use the templates on page 120 to cut out one circle for each flower from white paper. I used both large and small templates for different flowers in my cluster.

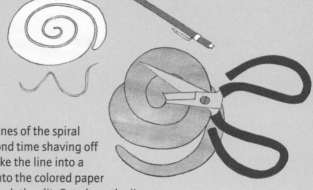

2 Make a pattern by cutting the lines of the spiral once and then go around a second time shaving off a very thin sliver of paper to make the line into a narrow slit. Place the pattern onto the colored paper and draw the spiral onto it through the slit. Cut along the line.

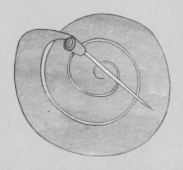

3 Begin to roll the spiral around the tip of the toothpick, starting with the outer end. The paper is easier to roll if you dampen the tip of the spiral first. Keep the paper as tightly rolled as you can and ease it around the toothpick. If you use paper that has color on only one side, roll so the color is on the inside—as the flower opens, you will get much more color.

Plain white paper

Pencil

Scissors

Solid color paper

Toothpick

White (PVA) glue

Green wire

Wire cutters

Thick needle or pin

Seed beads

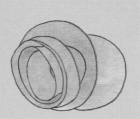

4 As you reach the end, remove the toothpick and let the shape unroll just a little.

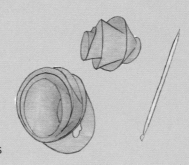

5 Place a dab of glue onto the inner end of the spiral at the bottom and position the coiled section on top of it. Push down gently into the middle of the coil so the bottom edges go into the glue. Hold gently until the glue dries.

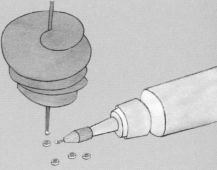

6 Cut a piece of wire to the length you want for the stem; I made mine 7in. (17.5cm) long. Make a hole through the base of the spiral with the needle. Push the wire up through the flower, put a dab of glue on the end and pick up a seed bead. I left my stamens quite long so the bead stands proud of the flower. Let dry.

7 Add a small dab of glue to the back of the flower to hold the flower steady in position on the wire stem.

Spray of CATKINS

Clusters of long, dangly catkins are easy to make. I used a snowflake-shaped punch to make my shapes because I wanted to cut quite a few, but you could roughly cut small circles of paper approximately ½in. (12mm) in diameter instead. Use different colors and weights of paper for the best effect.

1 Find a suitable branch or twig to use, or make your own from wire covered in brown tissue paper. Decide where to put your catkins and how many you need.

2 For each catkin, punch or cut out shapes from several different colors and thicknesses of paper and very thin cardstock. Punch out several at a time.

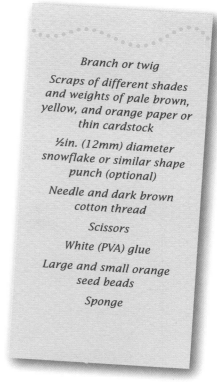

Branch or twig

Scraps of different shades and weights of pale brown, yellow, and orange paper or thin cardstock

½in. (12mm) diameter snowflake or similar shape punch (optional)

Needle and dark brown cotton thread

Scissors

White (PVA) glue

Large and small orange seed beads

Sponge

3 Cut an 18in. (45cm) length of thread, thread it onto the needle doubled and tie the ends into a knot. Put a dab of glue on the knot and thread a large seed bead down to the knot. Let dry.

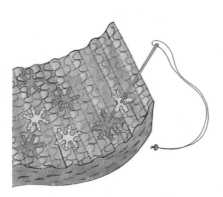

4 Put some of the punched shapes onto a sponge and pierce through the middle with the needle, pushing them onto the needle. Alternate colors at random.

5 Push a group of shapes onto the thread to about 1in. (2.5cm) above the bead. Smear a thin layer of glue onto the thread between the bead and the shapes. Before the glue dries, push the shapes down onto the glued thread towards the knot, spacing them out a little. Push another group of shapes to 1in. (2.5cm) above the first batch. Add glue to the thread and push the shapes down into it as before.

6 Continue gluing the thread and adding shapes until the catkin is the length you want—I made mine in several sizes from 3½in. (9cm) to 4½in. (11.5cm) long. Put a dab of glue on the top shape and thread a small seed bead onto the top. Wind the thread around a twig on the branch with approximately 1in. (2.5cm) of thread between the catkin and the twig so it dangles nicely. Glue the thread in place.

7 Glue the catkins in threes with varying lengths of thread between each catkin and the twig. Let dry and trim off any excess thread.

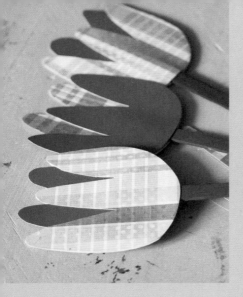

GRAPHIC
Tulips

These are pruned back to the simplest graphic shape and work best if the inner and outer petals are contrast colors or patterns. They stand up by themselves so there's no need for a vase, which makes them useful for narrow ledges—a cluster of them look great by a window.

1 Using the templates on page 120, for each tulip cut out a large and small leaf from paper and from thin cardstock that is rigid enough to hold the craft stick stem steady.

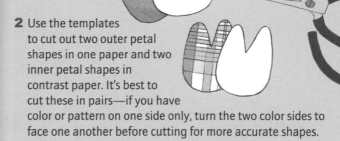

2 Use the templates to cut out two outer petal shapes in one paper and two inner petal shapes in contrast paper. It's best to cut these in pairs—if you have color or pattern on one side only, turn the two color sides to face one another before cutting for more accurate shapes.

3 Paint the craft stick stem and let dry. Place all four petal shapes pattern/color side down on your work surface. Cover the back of each petal with glue.

4 With an outer petal pattern/color side down, add an inner petal pattern/color side down on top. Glue the top 1in. (2.5cm) of the stem so it is centered onto the shape. Turn the remaining inner petal over so the pattern/color faces up and stick it onto the shape. Add the final outer petal in the same way. Try to keep the matching petals aligned. No matter how careful you are your shapes might not match exactly, but wait until the tulips are assembled and then trim off any excess so the shapes align perfectly.

5 Glue each paper leaf onto the back of a matching card leaf at the bottom only, beginning from where the leaves angle out. Score across each leaf twice where indicated.

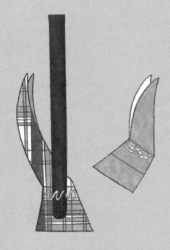

6 Place the larger leaf pair face side up and put glue across the width from A to B as marked on the template. Position the bottom of the stem in the center of the leaf, extending 1 in. (2.5cm) down from where the curve of the leaf begins, and then put a dab of glue on it. Glue the back of the smaller leaf pair from A to B as before, turn over and position on top of the larger leaf shape so the base section aligns exactly. Let dry.

7 Fold the base outward along the lower score line on either side to make a triangle to stand the tulip up. Pull both leaves slightly away from the stem along the upper score line.

⅛in. (3mm) wide quilling
paper strips in spring colors

Ruler

Scissors

White (PVA) glue

Hole punch

Scraps of yellow paper

Craft knife and cutting mat

Paper clip

LOOPY *flowers*

Looping paper strips can create wonderful flower shapes for festoons and vertical garlands; you get amazing shadow effects if you place them near a wall. They're a more sophisticated version of old-fashioned paper chains and simply brilliant for using up leftover strips. You can use very narrow strips, as I did, or wider ones for a much chunkier style.

1 For the small leaf shape use an ⅛in. (3mm) wide green strip approximately 16in. (40cm) long. Make a small loop and glue the end down to the strip. Turn the strip back on itself and make another loop opposite, to the same size. Glue where it meets the center.

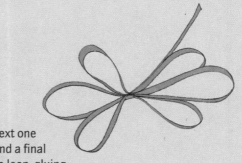

2 Make two more double loops, the next one a little larger than the one before and a final one the same size as the first double loop, gluing them in place as before.

3 Trim off any excess paper so the end of the last loop finishes in the middle. Let dry. Pinch the ends of the leaves into points. Make as many as you need—don't try to make them all exactly the same size and shape as they look quirkier if they are irregular.

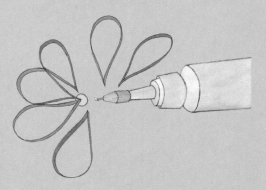

4 To make the flower base, use ten strips each 4in. (10cm) long—you can use all the same color, or mix two or more shades. Make each strip into a teardrop shape by gluing the two ends together.

5 Use the hole punch to cut a tiny yellow paper disk, put it down on the work surface and add a layer of glue. Arrange the teardrops in a circle, with their tips together on top of the yellow disk, adding a dab of glue to each tip and the sides where they touch each other. Let dry.

6 For the upper flower, use four strips each 8in. (20cm) long. Make each strip into a figure-of-eight shape by twisting one end of the strip over to the center to make a curved loop, and then bringing the other end over in the same way. Layer the figure-of-eight loops around into a flower and glue the centers together.

7 Put a dab of glue in the center of the flower base and stick the upper flower on top. Glue a second yellow disk into the center, using a toothpick to help you position it.

8 To make the flowers into a garland, cut 5in. (12.5cm) lengths of green for the stems. Fold across so one end is 1/8in. (3mm) longer than the other, then fold the longer end up so it overlaps the shorter one. Link the stems into the loop of a flower and into each other and then glue the 1/8in. (3mm) overlap closed, keeping the seams hidden. I linked every flower with three stems. Glue the leaves into the stems where you want them.

9 You can make a different version of these flowers by layering the shapes up in exactly the same way, but squeezing the tips of the petals into a point.

Chrysanthemums

These are a brilliant choice for using up odd rectangles of paper. They are so simple yet the flowers look so different when you use different textures, colors, and sizes of paper. You can make them flat as decorations or put them on stems for a vase display.

Envelopes, magazines, and brown paper

Strips of paper

Metal ruler

Masking tape

Craft knife and cutting mat

Glue stick

Thin tube or knitting needle

White (PVA) glue

Straws and wires

1 To make the black and white flower, open out the envelope and cut out a 10 x 5½in. (25 x 14cm) rectangle. Place it down on the cutting mat with the patterned inside facing upward and mask off 1in. (2.5cm) along each long edge. Cut vertical slits ¼in. (6mm) apart along the middle section between the masked off areas.

2 Cut out a second rectangle, this time 8 x 3½in. (20 x 9cm). Place it down on the cutting mat as before, mask off ¾in. (18mm) along each long edge, and cut vertical slits ¼in. (6mm) apart along the middle. Release both rectangles from the cutting mat and turn them over.

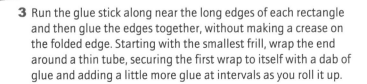

3 Run the glue stick along near the long edges of each rectangle and then glue the edges together, without making a crease on the folded edge. Starting with the smallest frill, wrap the end around a thin tube, securing the first wrap to itself with a dab of glue and adding a little more glue at intervals as you roll it up.

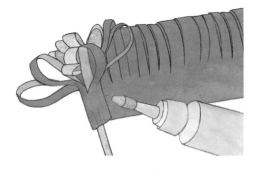

4 Glue the end and then add the larger frill around the outside in the same way, lining up the bases of the frills. Let dry.

5 Remove the tube or knitting needle for flat decorations. For a flower with a stem, add some glue to the top ½in. (12mm) of a clear plastic straw and push it up into the flower.

VARIATIONS

Cut out one 12 x 5½in. (30 x 14cm) rectangle from a magazine page for the outer frill. Mask off 1in. (2.5cm) along each long edge, and cut vertical slits ¼in. (6mm) apart. For the inner frill, cut out an 8 x 3½in. (20 x 9cm) rectangle from a magazine page. Mask off ¾in. (18mm) along each length, and cut vertical slits ⅛in. (3mm) apart. To make a covered stem, wrap a ¼in. (6mm) strip of magazine around a bamboo skewer.

For a smaller version, make one frill using a 9 x 3in. (23 x 7.5cm) rectangle cut from a magazine page, masking off ½in. (12mm) and with ⅛in. (3mm) cuts. Use a slender silver wire for a stem.

Seed PACKETS

What an extra special gift—lovely seeds from your garden in a bespoke packet. You can draw over flower images for the design but simplify the shapes because they don't need to represent the variety exactly; you can write the plant name on the outside. Adding the date the seeds were collected is also a good idea.

1 Using the template on page 120, cut out a packet shape in colored paper to 3½in. (9cm) wide by 4½in. (11.5cm) high. Choose which flower design to use or draw your own and transfer it onto the front panel. Cut out the shapes with a craft knife.

2 Place the front panel over a contrast color paper scrap and draw the outlines of the parts to be in this color lightly with pencil. Cut the shapes out slightly larger than the pencil marks, grouping as many together as possible on one piece of paper to make larger areas of color, and then erase the pencil lines.

3 Place the front panel right side up and slide the first colored shapes into position behind the cutouts, one piece at a time, to check they fit and do not cover cutouts that will be a different color. Turn the packet over and smear a little glue around the edge of the relevant holes.

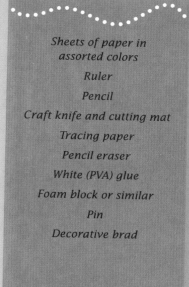

Sheets of paper in
assorted colors

Ruler

Pencil

Craft knife and cutting mat

Tracing paper

Pencil eraser

White (PVA) glue

Foam block or similar

Pin

Decorative brad

4 Turn the packet right side up and align the holes over the colored paper. Press lightly, turn over and let dry. Add other colors to the design in the same way. Lightly score the packet fold lines on the right side.

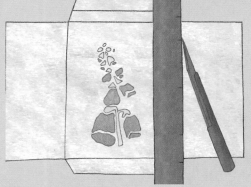

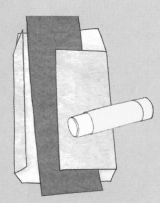

5 Place the packet right side down and put a piece of scrap paper over the center panel to protect it from any glue. Fold in the two sides, gluing the overlap. Fold up the bottom flap and glue. Let dry.

6 Put your seeds in the packet (put tiny seeds into a small bag first so they can't escape) and fold the top over twice. Place on a foam block to help you pierce a hole in the folded edge with a pin, before securing it with a pretty brad.

Oriental
POPPIES

These delicate flowers look equally effective made with smooth or crumpled paper. The technique is simple, the backs are not finished off, and there are no leaves, yet they still look very stylish—sometimes a very simple design is all you need. I used crystal beads for an extra bit of sparkle in the centers.

Tissue paper in oranges and yellows

Scissors

Pin

Thin green wire

White (PVA) glue

Crystal beads with a central hole large enough to fit over the wire

1 Using the large and small templates on page 121 cut out ten large petals for each flower, five in a strong color and five in a paler color, and five small petals in the darker color. It's easier to cut several at a time by folding the tissue paper up first. Pierce a hole in the base of each petal where indicated on the template.

2 Pair the large petals up, one dark with one pale. Slide a pair of petals onto the stem wire, with the darker one at the bottom, to approximately 1½in. (4cm) from the top. Put a little glue on the base of the petal and pinch it around the stem. This will help you position the other petals.

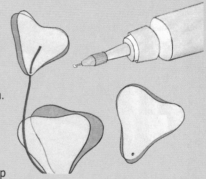

3 Slide the remaining petal pairs onto the stem from the bottom, turn the stem upside down and arrange the petals in a circle—the last pair of petals will overlap on both edges. Add a dab of glue to the base of the flower.

4 Squeeze the very ends of the petals firmly around the stem. As you squeeze the base with one hand, turn the flower the right way up and use your other hand to position the petals from inside the flower as well, before the glue dries completely.

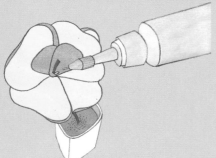

5 Add the small petals by pushing them down from the top of the stem, adding a tiny smear of glue to the base of the wire to hold them in place.

6 Squeeze a little glue into the hole of a bead and slide it onto the center wire. Trim off any excess wire, or you can leave it long as I did.

TIP

Fill a small jar with rice or small dried beans and stand the stem of the poppy in this while the glue dries.

Frilly FANCIES

This simple idea can be adapted to create a riot of different flowers; tiny mauve ones are reminiscent of chives whereas bright yellow ones remind me of Weyeriana or Japonica. They work best if you vary the color slightly, especially if pairs of flowers are very close together, because it helps separate the shapes. Plain green wire looks good for the stem; just choose a leaf color that matches.

Tissue paper in different yellows

Scissors

White (PVA) glue

Green wire for stems

Thin green cardstock

Masking tape

Pin

1 I made three slightly different stems and there are three flower sizes to choose from—the only things to remember are to arrange them with the smallest at the top, descending to the largest, and to vary the colors. A large flower uses four strips of 2 x 8in. (5 x 20cm) tissue; a medium one three strips of 1 ¾ x 8in. (4.5 x 20cm) tissue; a small one, three strips of 1 ½ x 5in. (4 x 12.5cm) tissue.

2 Make every flower in the same way. Arrange the strips for one flower on top of one another, fold over a couple of times, and cut a delicate frill three quarters of the way down into one edge.

3 Open out the stacked strips and roll the intact edge around the end of a spare piece of wire, using a dab of glue every now and then. Keep the layers on top of one another as much as you can. The frill has a tendency to splay out too early so try and hold it together. If it really gets out of control, simply break off part of the fringe, realign it, and glue it on again. Remove the flower from the wire. Let dry.

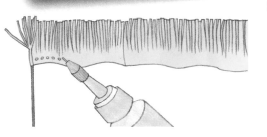

4 Using the template on page 121, cut out a series of double leaves in increasing sizes. Score a line down the middle of each leaf half and fold up the sides gently.

5 Plan out where you want your flowers and leaves to sit by laying them out along the wire stem. Mark the position of each double leaf with a little piece of masking tape.

6 Pierce through the center of the double leaf to make a hole large enough for the stem to slide through. Push all the leaves on at the bottom of the stem, beginning with the smallest, down to the largest. Move each double leaf up the stem into place, remove the tape and put a dab of glue above and below to hold in place.

7 Make a small vertical cut into the bottom "stalk" of each flower. Taking the first pair of flowers, slide the stem into the cut in one flower then glue the sides of the cut back together around the stem. Trim off any excess stalk, then add the second flower of the pair on the other side of the stem in the same way.

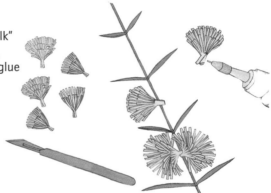

8 Fluff out the flowers and trim them into neater balls. Don't just snip around the edges. Angle the scissors into the flower and snip off tiny ends.

VARIATION

See how you can get differing effects by only using two colors of tissue paper. The chives don't even need leaves to embellish them.

Remember to cut crepe paper with scissors because a knife tends to drag it and it blunts the blade very quickly.

Daisy CHAINS

These pretty little chains can be looped around a mirror or draped around a table setting—you can use them individually or group several together. For speed you can buy a flower punch, but I enjoy making them from my own templates. Use string to join them for a softer look.

Thin white paper

Handmade mulberry paper in pale green

Craft knife and cutting mat

Sponge

Pin and toothpick

Thin silver-colored wire and wire cutters

White (PVA) glue

Yellow tissue paper

Round-nosed pliers

1 Using the templates on page 121 cut out ten large and ten small flowers from white paper and 20 flower backs from pale green. Put the flowers onto a sponge and make an indent along the length of each petal by pressing the back of a craft knife or piece of thin wire along it.

2 Cut ten 5in. (12.5cm) lengths of wire for the stems. Bend each wire into a gentle curve. Cut ten strips of pale green paper, ¼in. (6mm) wide and approximately 10in. (25cm) long. Smear a little glue on the back of a strip and wrap it around the wire at an angle of 45 degrees to cover it. Trim off the excess and let dry. Cover all the stems the same way.

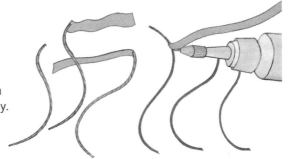

3 Glue two green backs together for each flower, then pierce a hole in the centre with something large enough so the wire will go through easily; I used a pin and then a cocktail stick to widen it. Push a green back onto each wire for 1 in. (2.5cm) or so. Pierce a hole in the center of a pair of flowers and slide them down the stem, so they are slightly above the green back.

4 Tear off nine thumb-sized pieces of yellow tissue paper for each large daisy and five for each small one. Pierce a hole through one set and push them onto the wire. Make a small circle at one end of the wire with the round-nosed pliers and bend it over at a right angle to the wire. Repeat for the other flowers.

5 With a little diluted glue between your thumb and forefinger, scrunch the yellow tissue paper around the wire circle to form a loose ball. Repeat for the other flowers. Push the flowers back up to the yellow ball while it is still tacky. Add a little glue behind the flower and slide the green back up to it.

6 Arrange the daisies in a circle; I alternated the sizes. Make a small loop at the end of one stem, making sure it is a complete circle otherwise the daisies will fall out. Thread a daisy stem through this and make a loop at the end of that stem. Keep threading and making loops until the last daisy, then twist the last stem around the first to complete the chain. Bend and tweak the wires if you want to alter how the daisies fall.

VARIATIONS

The daisy chain could just be hung down in a straight line or looped along like bunting—make the chain in exactly the same way but do not join the ends. Or consider making the flowers in a bright color for a different look.

Falling leaf
POMPOMS

I can't remember the first time I made these because it was so long ago. They are super simple and, just because they've been around forever, they don't need to look dated! Choose delicate colors and layer the tissue in different combinations for different effects. The pompoms look beautiful suspended on invisible thread with leaves trailing down.

Tissue paper in pale lemon, pinks, and green

Scissors

Strip of cardstock

Craft knife and cutting mat

Fine wire

Wire cutters and pliers

Thin tube

Invisible nylon thread

Needle

White (PVA) glue

1 For a 6in. (15cm) diameter pompom, cut nine pieces of tissue paper each 6in. (15cm) square. Stack the squares neatly in a pile and smooth them out. Cut a strip of card measuring 1 x 9in. (2.5 x 22.5cm), or use a ruler instead.

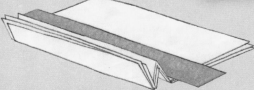

2 Place the cardstock strip along one edge of the stacked paper and, using it to help keep the paper rigid, flip it backwards and forwards to pleat the tissue into equal accordion folds. Remove the cardstock.

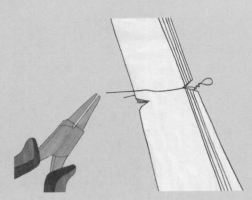

3 Using the craft knife, cut a small "V" into either side of middle of the folded paper strip. Cut a 4in. (10cm) length of wire and make a loop in the center by folding it around a thin tube and twisting the strands once. Place the wire around the middle of the folded paper strip and twist the ends together.

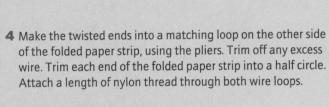

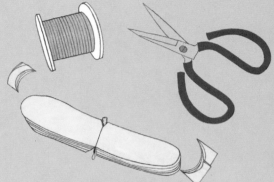

4 Make the twisted ends into a matching loop on the other side of the folded paper strip, using the pliers. Trim off any excess wire. Trim each end of the folded paper strip into a half circle. Attach a length of nylon thread through both wire loops.

5 Now for the fun bit. The paper is very delicate so it is best if you work on a tabletop. Lay the folded strip at a right angle to you and turn it on its edge. Working on the half that is furthest away from you, first fan out the end. Then tease out the layers, one layer at a time and very, very gently, pulling them one by one away from the center.

6 When you have finished one side, take the shape in your hands and separate the layers on the other side in the same way until you have created a rounded pompom.

7 Cut out several leaves using the top leaf template on page 125 and fold them in half—I used mainly green with a few lemon leaves. Using a needle, thread the base of the leaves onto one end of the nylon thread, spacing them out, then add a dab of glue to each and squeeze them into place on the thread.

TIP

Larger pompoms will need more layers of paper—I used 14 layers when I made a 10in. (25cm) diameter version. You may need to cut a small slit down each segment to help the paper spread out more.

NAPKIN VARIATION

Napkins are often in 2-ply paper. Find a pattern you like and pull the layers carefully apart—you will be able to make both plain and patterned pompoms from just one napkin. The larger the pompom, the more sheets of paper you need to make it look nice and full. So, depending on how thin your paper is, you may want to add or subtract a few sheets as necessary.

Chapter 2

BRIGHT AND BEAUTIFUL

Anemones

I made these in different colors to tie around napkins or to use as markers for the stems of wine glasses and they made a great visual impact. They are attached with a bow tied from a short length of raffia, so if you want to use the flowers for something else later you can just cut the raffia off.

1 For each flower cut ten crepe paper petals with the grain of the paper lying vertical to the petal as shown (see template on page 121). I cut several out in one go by folding up a strip of crepe paper and cutting through all the layers.

2 Dampen the petals with water and flatten them on a plastic board. Swirl a wet paintbrush in your chosen color then dilute the color by dipping the paintbrush into clean water. Stroke some color onto the top third of each petal—it will seep down into the rest of the petal slightly. Add slightly deeper color around the very top edge if you want a more intense color. Have a piece of kitchen towel ready to dab off excess paint if necessary. Let dry.

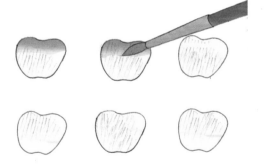

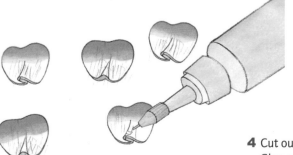

3 Stretch the wide ends of the petals out with your fingers to make them into more of a bowl shape. Stack the petals in pairs, place a dab of glue in the middle of the narrow end and make a small pleat at this end to accentuate the bowl shape.

4 Cut out a ⅝in. (15mm) diameter circle from thin white cardstock. Glue pairs of petals, overlapping one another slightly, around the edge of the circle.

White crepe paper
strip

Pencil

Scissors

Plastic board or
cutting mat

Watercolors and
paintbrush

Absorbent kitchen towel

White (PVA) glue

Scraps of thin white and
green cardstock

Black tissue paper

Black paper

Raffia

5 Roll some scraps of kitchen towel into a ¾in. (18mm) diameter ball. Cut a 5in. (12.5cm) square of black tissue paper and fold it twice to form a smaller square. Wrap it around the ball and twist the ends together tightly to secure. Cut the ends off close to the ball but without revealing any white paper underneath. Dab some glue on the cut ends to hold the tissue in place. Let dry.

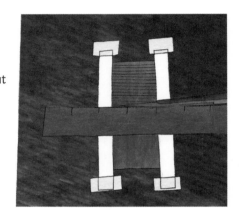

6 Cut a rectangle of black paper 4 x 2½in. (10 x 6.5cm) and mask off a strip ½in. (12mm) wide down each long side. Cut slits at ⅛in. (3mm) intervals between the masked areas. Gently fold the strip over in half lengthwise, without creasing the slit edge, and glue the intact edges together.

7 Make small cuts into the intact edge every three or four slits but do not cut through the frill completely. Making the cut end of the ball the top, glue the fringe around the bottom third of the ball, overlapping the small cuts to help wrap it around.

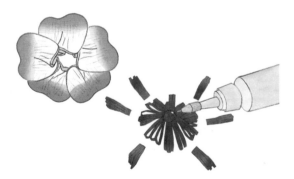

8 Cut off excess fringe when you have completed one circle of the ball. Trim the remainder into three or four pieces and glue those randomly around the outside, to cover any gaps. Cut through the top of a few of the loops nearest the ball in the center. Glue the fringed center into the petal circle.

9 Cut a 12in. (30cm) strip of raffia and glue the center of the strip to the back of the white cardstock circle. Cut out a ⅝in. (15mm) diameter circle from thin green cardstock and glue this on top of the white cardstock over the raffia. Let dry.

Cupcake POPPIES

Look out for cupcake liners that have a different color inside and out because they are so versatile for these flowers. The paper does tend to tear quite easily, so be very gentle as you stretch the liners out.

1 To make one bloom, take two mini liners and make an equal number of slits through the ruffled edge, stopping at the flat center.

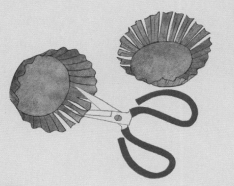

Small pink cupcake liners, approximately 2½in. (6.5cm) top diameter

Mini dark brown cupcake liners, approximately 1¾in. (4.5cm) top diameter

Scissors

Toothpick

White (PVA) glue

Pencil

Ruler

Craft knife and cutting mat

Pin

Thin wire and pliers

Dark brown buttons (optional)

2 On the first liner, roll every spoke tightly around a toothpick towards the center. Repeat on alternate spokes only of the second liner. Glue the first liner into the center of the second one to make the middle of the poppy.

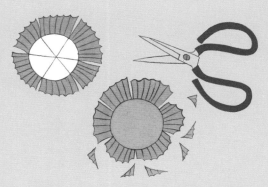

3 Using the front template on page 121, cut six equidistant slits around two of the pink liners, from the edge to the flat center. Flatten each liner out and cut off the edges of the six segments to form rounded petals.

4 On a third pink liner, use the template to make six cuts as before, but trim each segment down by approximately one third before trimming them into smaller petals.

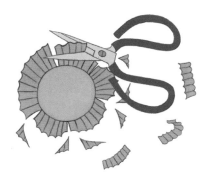

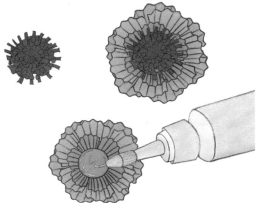

5 Glue the smaller petals into one of the bigger pink liners—you do need a color variation here so turn the smaller petals inside out if you can. Glue this duo onto the second large pink liner, then glue the middle in and let dry.

6 Using the back template on page 121, divide a mini liner into seven segments to make the flower back. Cut off one segment, then extend the slit at one side to the middle of the liner. Overlap the edges at the center and glue in so the segments are all adjoining and the base of the flower back forms a cone. Trim the segments into triangles and use a pin to make a hole in the center of the cone.

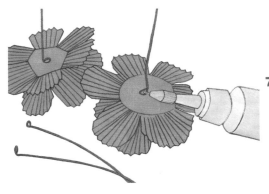

7 Cut a piece of wire to the length of stem you want and make a small loop in one end, turning the loop to a right angle with the stem. Glue the loop to the back of the poppy. Let dry.

8 Put a small dab of glue on the inside of each triangle of the flower back and slide the shape down the wire to sit against the back of the flower.

9 To finish off the center of the flower on the front you can add a dark button with a dab of glue if you like, but this is optional.

Flowering Cactus
LIGHTS

Try grouping several of these together on a bed of fine gravel or stones. Or, if you have enough balloons, make a huge group of assorted sizes as a dramatic focal point. Keep the layers of paper quite thin so the light will show through well.

Balloons

Wide mouth candlestick or other suitable container

White (PVA) glue

White packing paper

Rubber gloves (optional)

String

Scissors

Green tissue paper in different shades

Pin

Scalpel and cutting mat

Bright color paper in pink and green

⅛in. (3mm) wide quilling strips in pink, yellow, and lilac

Quilling tool or toothpick

Round end pencil or chopstick

LED fairy lights

Gravel

1 For each small cactus, blow up a balloon to approximately 2½in. (6.5cm) tall. Balance the balloon on the candlestick or other suitable container to make it easier to manage—you need to be able to paste the paper quite close to the bottom of the balloon.

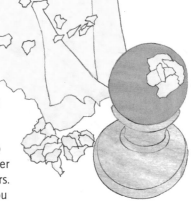

2 Make a thin glue paste by mixing some white (PVA) glue 1:2 with water—you won't need much so only make a small amount. Tear the packing paper into very small irregular pieces. Put a piece of paper onto the balloon and smear a thin layer of paste over it, using your fingers. You can wear rubber gloves if you need to.

3 Continue to build up pieces of base paper onto the balloon with a little glue between layers until the balloon is completely covered almost up to the base. Let dry.

SAFETY TIP

Be safety aware and use only low temperature lights, such as LEDs—if you are worried, only put lamps under the larger cacti.

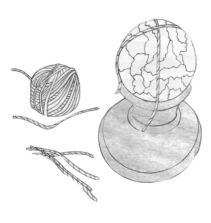

4 Cut eight lengths of string approximately 4in. (10cm) long. Glue lines of string to make radiating spokes from the top of the cactus to its base.

5 Turn the cactus upside down and continue gluing the string to the paper only, so the ends of string overlap at the bottom. Let dry.

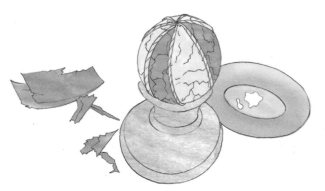

6 Take two different tones of green tissue paper and tear them into small pieces. Using your fingers again, smear a thin layer of paste onto alternate sections of the cactus and layer on one color of green. Let dry. Cover the remaining segments with the other color green. Let dry.

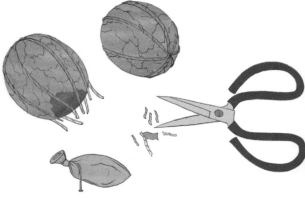

7 Pierce the balloon and remove it from the cactus shell. Trim off the bottom of the cactus and the extra string so the cactus will stand up properly.

8 For the flowers, cut out a 6in. (15cm) x ¾in. (18mm) strip of pink paper and two 4¼in. (10.5cm) x ½in. (12mm) strips of green. Use a scalpel to cut a zigzag into one edge of each, leaving an uncut strip ⅛in. (3mm) wide on the opposite long edge. Slide a quilling strip into the slot at the end of the quilling tool and roll a tight coil using a 24in. (60cm) strip of pink and 24in. (60cm) strip of yellow. Make two smaller coils, each using a 6in. (15cm) strip of yellow and a 6in. (15cm) strip of lilac.

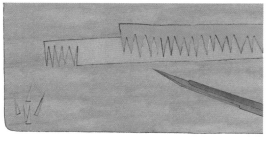

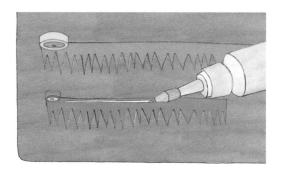

9 Put a thin strip of glue along the intact edge of each zigzag strip. Roll the pink strip around the large coil and a green strip around each small coil. Push the frilled edges outward.

10 Gently push the rounded end of a pencil or a chopstick into the center of each coil to create an indent. Smear a little glue on the back to keep each flower in shape and glue them at random onto the cactus.

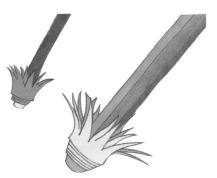

11 Make the larger cactus in the same way, but start with the balloon blown up to 5in. (12.5cm) tall, and make more of the flowers in each size. Arrange the lights on a bed of small gravel, covering the wire with the stones, and position a cactus over each lamp.

Lollipop FLOWERS

These are an edible treat as well as a visual one—they are such fun to give because the lollipop can be removed, leaving the flower intact. Perfect for young and old, you can tailor them to favorite comic characters by using appropriate printed paper.

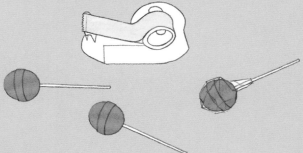

Round lollipops

Cellophane

Clear sticky tape

Printed wrapping paper

Scissors

Thin tube or knitting needle

White (PVA) glue

Craft knife and cutting mat

Paper straws large enough to hold the lollipop stick snugly

1 Remove the wrapper and cover the lollipop with 4in. (10cm) square of cellophane—it looks prettier if you can see its color. Secure the cellophane very firmly around the stick with clear sticky tape.

TIP

If the paper you want to use is too flimsy to hold a good shape make the outer flower in stiffer paper. I found some wonderful double-sided wrapping paper to use.

2 Using the templates on page 122, for each lollipop cut out one outer flower and two smaller inner flowers. Snip right to the center hole between two of the petals and then roll the outer edge of every petal around a thin tube to form a soft curve. Any pattern or color you want to feature should be uppermost with the petals curling underneath.

3 Make the outer flower into a cone shape by overlapping the last petal halfway over the first one. Secure with a dab of glue and hold until dry.

4 Make the two inner flowers in the same way as the outer one, but overlap one of them by one and a half petals and the other by two and a half petals, adding glue and holding until dry. The featured pattern or color side should always be on the inside of the cone with the petals curling outward.

5 Add some glue around the inner center of the outer flower and push the middle-sized flower down into it. Add glue around the inner center of the middle-sized flower and push the smallest flower in. Be careful not to get glue into the central hole. Let dry.

6 Cut six 1 in. (2.5cm) long slits into one end of the straw. Push the end down on a firm surface to push the spokes out into a starfish shape. Add glue to the inside of the spokes and push the starfish onto the back of the flower, lining up the flower center with the hole in the straw.

7 Push the stick of the lollipop through the center of the flower and well down into the straw.

8 You can also make these with a single foil-wrapped chocolate as the flower center instead of a lollipop— although hardly anyone will be able to resist eating it for long! The flowers look stylish in white and you can add a tiny hint of color by gluing on small color dots. To keep the flower afterward, tear the foil wrapper open at the front to remove the chocolate and then scrunch the foil up again as the flower center.

Waterlilies

You can experiment with colored pencils and parchment paper but I find tracing paper and soft chalks will give you a wonderful and subtle translucent flower. Of course tracing paper really does not stretch but you can still get it to curve gently. These look magnificent as a gift decoration but can easily be made into a table decoration by adding leaves and stems. They work best on a white background, such as a white platter, or a mirrored surface to look as though they are floating.

Tracing paper

Scissors

Thin tube

Chalks in pinks, mauves, yellow, and greens

Q-tips

Spray fixative

White (PVA) glue

Clear tape

Scalloped-blade scissors (optional)

Toothpick

Green pencil

Craft knife and cutting mat

1 For the largest flower, cut six petals in each of four sizes from tracing paper using the templates on page 122. Imagine the petal as a diamond shape and roll each of the four sides around a thin tube to make soft curves all round, but be careful not to tear the paper at the circle edge. Use your thumbnail to make a curved angle at the base of the petal where it joins the circle.

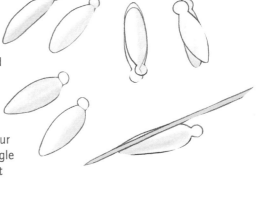

2 Build up the color layers on the petals gradually to get a subtle effect by gently using a Q-tip to rub the chalk in. Do not color the base circle. Spray the color carefully with fixative. Let dry.

TIPS

Don't handle tracing paper too much because grease from your fingers may cause the color to be patchy. When rolling edges, try to touch only the petal back.

Cutting shapes from tracing paper is easier if you sandwich it between scrap paper.

3 Arrange the six largest petals in a flower shape, stacking the base circles and fixing them together with glue. Let dry. Continue to glue on layers of six petals in descending size, letting them dry before you add another layer.

TIP

The last petal on each circle will overlap the petals on both sides. Start each circle of petals in a different place.

4 Cut a 2in. (5cm) diameter circle from tracing paper and color it yellow or white with the chalks as before. Use scalloped-edged scissors to cut around the edge if you have them, or trim a scalloped edge freehand. Cut a slit on either side of each scallop, down toward the center of the circle for approximately 1½in. (4cm). Curl the spokes around a toothpick toward the center. Glue into the middle of the flower.

5 For a stem version with leaves, using the templates on page 122 cut, color, and fix the leaf and stem shapes as in steps 1–2, using green chalks. Extend the stem height for some flowers, so they will sit at different levels. On the leaves, draw some veins on first using colored pencil before adding the chalk color.

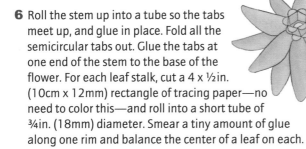

6 Roll the stem up into a tube so the tabs meet up, and glue in place. Fold all the semicircular tabs out. Glue the tabs at one end of the stem to the base of the flower. For each leaf stalk, cut a 4 x ½in. (10cm x 12mm) rectangle of tracing paper—no need to color this—and roll into a short tube of ¾in. (18mm) diameter. Smear a tiny amount of glue along one rim and balance the center of a leaf on each.

TIP

If you make several flowers, extend the plain middle part of the stem to make it taller so the stems will be longer for some flowers, and vary the height of the leaf stalks.

TRIPLE *Pinks*

Coffee filters have a very good texture and weight for these carnation-style flowers. I glue a lightweight crepe streamer strip on the inside edges of the filters to make the flower that much fuller. You'll notice some subtle differences between my flowers but they are all made using the same papers and felt tip pen. Try putting water above the pen line to keep the filter edge white or swapping the layers around.

Size 2 white coffee filters

Scissors and scissors with zigzag blades

1¾in. (4.5cm) wide white crepe paper streamer

White (PVA) glue

Pink tissue

Water-soluble pink felt-tip pen

Waterproof board

Water and paintbrush

Elastic bands

Wire for stem, already covered with paper

White crepe paper

Spray adhesive

1 Each flower uses three filters. Tear off the side and bottom seam of each, fold twice into a smaller segment and cut a zigzag edge along the top. Trim off the bottom into a semicircle.

2 Cut 17in. (42.5cm) length of crepe streamer, fold the length over and over to make a small rectangle and cut a zigzag across the top edge. Open out the length and glue it around the inside top edge of the first filter so it stands proud by ⅛in. (3mm). Pleat the very bottom edge of the crepe streamer as you glue it to make it fit around the curve. Trim off a curve at the two top corners through all layers using the zigzag scissors.

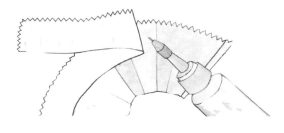

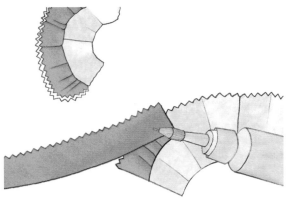

3 Cut a long strip of pink tissue paper 1¾in. (4.5cm) deep, cut a zigzag along one long side and use it to make an edging on the inside top edge of the second filter in the same way as in step 2. Then add a second edging on the outside top edge of the filter, using another length of crepe streamer as in step 2.

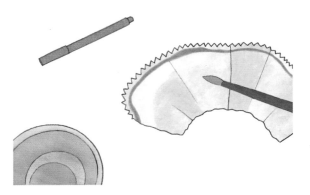

4 On the third filter, trim off a curve at the two top corners using the zigzag scissors. Using the felt-tip pen, draw an ⅛in. (3mm) thick line ¼in. (6mm) down from the top edge. Put the filter on a waterproof surface and brush a line of clean water just underneath the felt-tip line so the color bleeds nicely. Add more water if necessary to make the color bleed right up to the top edge. Let dry.

5 Make another crepe paper edge on the inside top edge of the third filter in the same way as step 2, but this time position it slightly below the filter edge.

TIP

Practice brushing water over the felt-tip line on a spare piece first to gauge the effect you get.

TIP

When rolling, place an elastic band under the flower head at each stage to hold the shape, replacing it with a strip of masking tape when you are ready for the next stage.

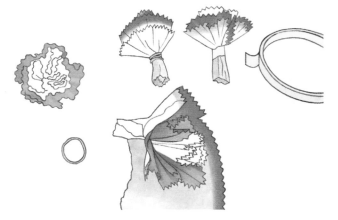

6 To make the flower center roll the first filter up, with the crepe paper outside, pleating the bottom edge from time to time as you roll. Hold the shape firmly at the bottom. Add the second filter next, with the pink tissue on the inside. Add the third filter last, with the crepe on the outside.

7 Cut the covered wire to the stem length you want and paint it green with a little watercolor. Make three slight angles along the stem for a more natural look. Trim the flower base to 1in. (2.5cm) and push the stem firmly up into the flower.

8 Cut two pieces of crepe paper each large enough to make a double leaf (see template on page 122) and stick together with spray adhesive. Paint the paper on both sides with some diluted green watercolor. Cut another piece of crepe paper 2 x 3in. (5 x 7.5cm) and paint that. When dry, cut out the double leaf and snip some irregular triangles out of the top and bottom edges of the base.

9 Cover the masking tape under the flower head with glue and mold the base shape around it.

10 Pierce a large enough hole in the centre of the double leaf for the stem to fit through. Place a dab of glue on the stem at the top angle and push the leaf up to it. Pinch the leaf around the stem to hold it in place. Curve the ends of the double leaf outward over a toothpick.

Topiary CONES

A group of topiary cones forms a stunning table centerpiece, or just one cone perched on a pile of napkins also looks great. If you pin your shapes to the cone instead of gluing them, you can reuse the foam cone base for something else later. Use shades of one color paper, or add a contrast color as I have done.

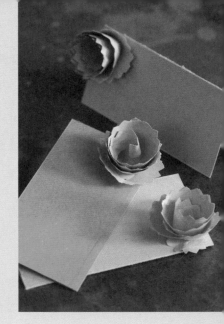

6 x 3in. (15 x 7.5cm)
foam cone

Green paper in two shades

Pale pink paper

Scrap paper

Scissors

Zigzag scissors

White (PVA) glue

Toothpick

Pins

1 Make a couple of practice foliage spirals first. Using the small spiral template on page 120, cut one circle out using zigzag scissors, but then cut the spiral inside it using ordinary scissors.

2 Now cut only the upper edge of the spiral, again using the zigzag scissors. What will become the base of the foliage needs to remain flat.

3 Begin to roll the coil around the tip of the toothpick, starting with the end of the outer spiral and with the zigzag edge at the top. The paper is easier to roll if you dampen the tip of the spiral first. Keep the paper as tight as you can and ease it around the toothpick until you reach the end.

4 As you reach the end, remove the toothpick and let the shape unroll just a little. Place a dab of glue onto the inner end of the spiral at the bottom and position the coiled section on top of it. Push down gently into the middle of the coil so the bottom edges go into the glue. Hold gently until the glue firms.

TIP

The coils can be time consuming to construct so you won't want to waste any! If you have some left over, cut out 3in. (7.5cm) square pieces of thin card, fold in the middle and stick a spiral in one corner to make coordinating place name cards.

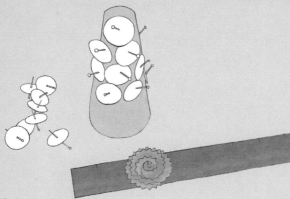

5 Measure the diameter of your practice coil and cut out several circles the same size from scrap paper. Pin them on to your cone to work out how many foliage coils you will need to cover it. Plan out how many you want to make in each color.

6 Make as many coils as you need. Push a pin through the centre from front to back and pin each coil onto the cone. Begin at the top and gradually work outward—it's easy to pull the coils out and reposition them if you need to.

Grape
HYACINTHS

You can make these by cutting out your own paper strips from colored paper if you want, but I think they are even prettier if you can track down some pearlized quilling paper strips. I found some miniature plant pots as the perfect finishing touch.

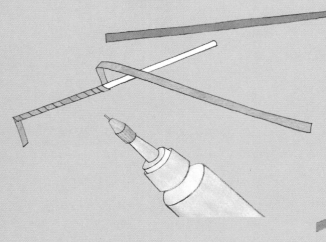

1 Make a light pencil mark half way down a lollipop stick. Leaving a tail of approximately ½in. (12mm) at one end, put a light smear of glue along a 12in. (30cm) strip of pale violet quilling paper and wrap it around the stick at an angle of approximately 45 degrees until you reach the pencil mark. Trim off the strip at right angles.

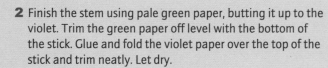

2 Finish the stem using pale green paper, butting it up to the violet. Trim the green paper off level with the bottom of the stick. Glue and fold the violet paper over the top of the stick and trim neatly. Let dry.

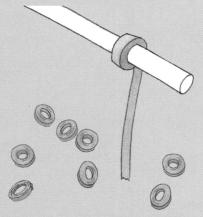

3 Each flower head has 20 open center coils in pale violet: five from a 24in. (60cm) strip, five from a 20in. (50cm) strip, five from a 16in. (40cm) strip, and five from a 12in. (30cm) strip. Wrap the quilling paper tightly around the ¼in. (6mm) diameter tube, trying to keep each layer on top of each other. Use a dab of glue to complete the first circle and hold the paper in place, and add another dab of glue to the tail as you finish rolling. Tap the coils on a flat surface to tidy them up and squeeze one end of each to make into a teardrop shape.

4in. (10cm) long by ⅛in. (3mm) diameter paper lollipop sticks

24in. (60cm) long by ⅛in. (3mm) wide pearlized quilling paper strips in pale violet, pale green, and dark violet

White (PVA) glue

¼in. (6mm) diameter tube

Scissors

Quilling tool or toothpick

Craft knife and cutting mat

Masking tape and small box

Miniature plant pot

White watercolor paint and paintbrush

Sticky tack

Small amount of fake moss

Pencil

Ruler

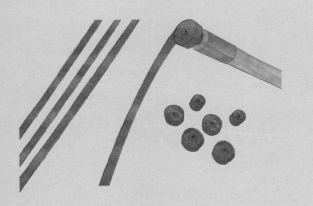

4 Each flower head has 15 closed center coils in dark violet: five from a 16in. (40cm) strip, five from a 12in. (30cm), and five from a 6in. (15cm) strip. Use a quilling tool or toothpick to roll the coils very tightly right from the center, trying to keep each layer on top of each other. Glue and tap the coils as before, but no need to squeeze the end.

TIP

A quilling tool has a metal prong with a slit in the end to thread the end of a paper strip into, so you can roll it up tightly. You can use a toothpick instead, but keep the strips coiled as tightly as possible as you work.

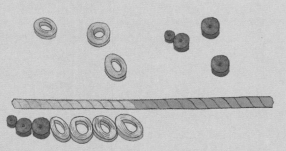

5 Put the stem onto a plastic surface, like a cutting mat. Arrange a row of coils in a straight line along the violet end in size order, with the top coil slightly above the end of the stem and the ovals at an angle. Glue the coils to each other with little dabs of glue, starting with the largest; it's easier to stick them one at a time.

6 Make four more rows of coils in the same way. Let dry and then glue the first row to the stem. Let dry.

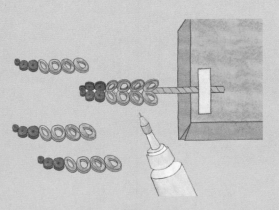

7 Tape the green end of the stem to something so the flower head is held in the air and rotate it a little less than 90 degrees. Attach another row of coils with tiny dabs of glue as before—your aim is to get five rows of coils around the stem so the entire head is covered, letting each row dry before rotating and adding the next.

8 Cut 8in. (20cm), 7in. (17.5cm), 6in. (15cm), and 4in. (10cm) lengths of pale green quilling paper and trim each end into a long, slim triangle. Score each strip in half lengthwise and fold, using the back of a craft knife or needle to help ease the crease. Fold across the width so each side is an uneven length, keeping the center lengthwise crease on the outside.

9 Distress the flowerpot by dabbing it with a little white paint. Put some sticky tack into the flowerpot and arrange the flower and leaves in it. Cover the sticky tack with some fake moss.

Origami FLOWERS

These are not made using origami techniques, but I am taking full advantage of the fabulous patterns the paper comes in. These flowers look their best when you use double-sided paper because you can see both inside and the outside of the flower very clearly. The origami paper I used was only patterned on one side, so I lined it with some tissue paper, which also helped to strengthen the shape.

Thin green wire in two different thicknesses

Wire cutters and round-nosed pliers

Tissue paper in chestnut color

White (PVA) glue

Origami paper at least 4½in. (11.5cm) square

Tissue paper to coordinate with origami paper (optional)

Spray adhesive (optional)

Scissors

Scalloped-blade scissors (optional)

Masking tape

Pin

Thin tube or knitting needle

Dark green paper

Craft knife and cutting mat

1 Cut five 3in. (7.5cm) lengths of thinner wire for stamens and one 18in. (45cm) length of thicker wire for the stem. Cut some ¼in. (6mm) wide lengths of chestnut color tissue paper. Leaving a short tail, wrap the tissue paper at an angle of 45 degrees around each wire to cover it, adding a dab of glue every now and then. Let dry. Tidy up the ends.

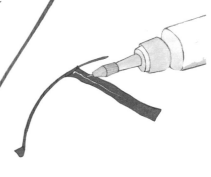

2 If necessary, back the sheets of origami paper with colored tissue paper using a light coating of spray adhesive.

TIPS

I used a slightly thicker wire for the stem because I wanted it to be more rigid.

Position the flower templates on the paper first to make sure they fit, and save any scraps after cutting.

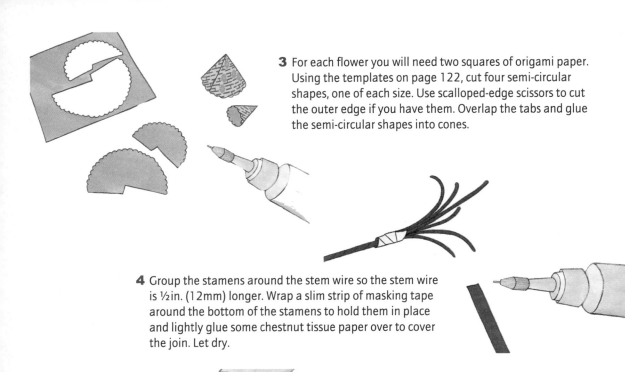

3 For each flower you will need two squares of origami paper. Using the templates on page 122, cut four semi-circular shapes, one of each size. Use scalloped-edge scissors to cut the outer edge if you have them. Overlap the tabs and glue the semi-circular shapes into cones.

4 Group the stamens around the stem wire so the stem wire is ½in. (12mm) longer. Wrap a slim strip of masking tape around the bottom of the stamens to hold them in place and lightly glue some chestnut tissue paper over to cover the join. Let dry.

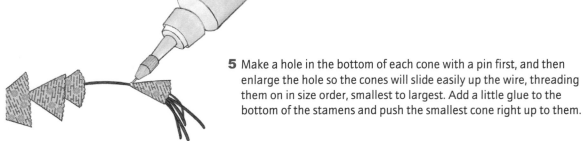

5 Make a hole in the bottom of each cone with a pin first, and then enlarge the hole so the cones will slide easily up the wire, threading them on in size order, smallest to largest. Add a little glue to the bottom of the stamens and push the smallest cone right up to them.

6 Position the other cones along the stem, leaving a space of approximately ½in. (12mm) between each. Try and get all the seams along one side. When you have each in its correct place, add a little dab of glue to the inside and outside of the base of the cone. Hold the cone in place with your fingers for at least a couple of minutes until the glue starts to set, then you can put the stem into a vase while it continues to set. Let dry before gluing the next cone.

7 For the leaf cut out an 11in. (28cm) long isosceles triangle, 1in. (2.5cm) wide at the base tapering to a point, from dark green paper. Score the leaf lengthwise and fold. Open out and curve the leaf back on itself by rolling it around a tube or knitting needle.

8 Fold the base of the leaf around a toothpick, and glue the bottom open edges together just in the corner. Let dry and trim the corner off into a curve. Remove the toothpick and slide the stem down into the leaf.

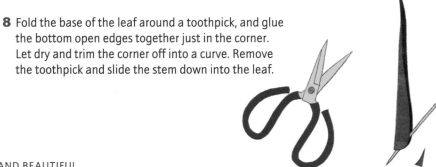

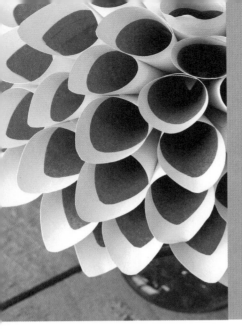

Vibrant DAHLIAS

It's hard to choose colors for these but I experimented and found it was worth the extra effort to make a colored inner petal, and I also used different shades to add extra interest. The flowers need a surprising number of petals and it's worth taking the time to make a cone as a "form" because this will really help make the petals more accurate. If you are having difficulty fitting petals together, try rolling a few slimmer ones.

1 Using the template on page 123 make a cone from very thin cardstock to use as a form to wrap your petals around—it will make the process much easier and faster.

2 My flower took 93 petals—for each layer from top to bottom: 6, 10, 13, 15, 18, 21, 10. It is always better to make a few extra petals in case you have a few accidents. Using the templates on page 123, cut the outer petal as many times as you need in white paper and the same number of inner petals in colored tissue paper.

3 Roll one white petal into a cone, using the guidelines on the template to see where to align the edges, and tape it. Position the cone onto the form and draw around the edges, also marking where the overlap occurs. Use these lines as a guide when making other petals.

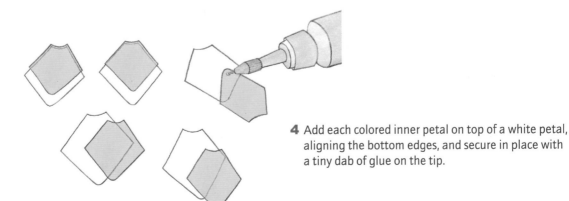

4 Add each colored inner petal on top of a white petal, aligning the bottom edges, and secure in place with a tiny dab of glue on the tip.

Thin cardstock

Pencil

Ruler

Scissors

White (PVA) glue

Thin white paper

Colored tissue paper

Clear sticky tape

Toothpick

Craft knife and
cutting mat

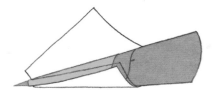

5 Roll a petal with its liner into a cone over the form, but don't tape it yet. Open out the white sides so the colored liner makes a complete cone, then roll the white sides back into position over the top. If you don't do this, you may get strips of white appearing where they shouldn't. Seal with a piece of clear sticky tape in the middle of the overlap.

TIPS

Always roll the petals on the form in the same order, so they overlap the same way.

Make sure you put the tape in the middle, and not at the end, so it will be hidden when the petals are in place.

6 Make enough petals for two complete circles, approximately 21 for the base layer and 18 for the second. Cut a 4in. (10cm) diameter circle from thin white card and draw a 1½in. (4cm) diameter circle in the center. Glue on the base layer of petals with the bottom ends facing towards the center and aligned with the center circle. Glue the second layer of petals on top with their bottom ends slightly overlapping those of the base layer.

7 Make approximately 15 petals for the third layer and snip ⅛in. (3mm) off the end. Glue the third layer in place, again with their bottom ends slightly further into the center circle than the previous layer.

8 By the fourth layer you will have got the hang of making the petals so there is no need to glue the liners in place first. The petals need to be smaller now so cut an extra ¼in. (6mm) off the end of each petal and liner before you roll them up. Use the form to roll them as before but align them at the bottom, not on the guidelines.

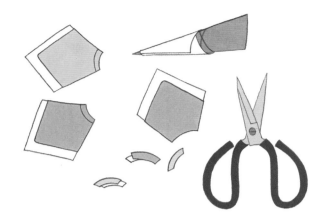

9 The petals for the fifth layer are the same size as for the fourth layer. To fit these on, you will need to cut the bottom of the cone into a "V" shape.

10 Arrange five or six petals in the center attractively. Continue to trim the bottom to fit and cut it into a "V" to slot them in.

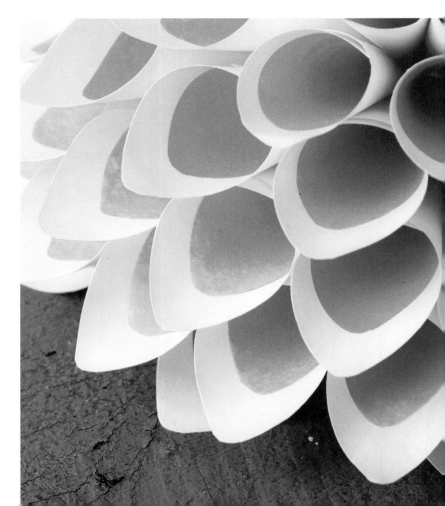

11 Take another 10 petals the original size as for the base layer and glue these under the card circle, but further inside so they are set back from the outer edge of the base layer.

Colorful GERBERA

Big, bold, and beautiful, these are quick to make once you have cut the shapes out and rolling the petals around a straw gets easier with practice. You need to use quite a thick stem because the base of the flower can become rather large.

1 You can use either crepe paper streamers or crepe paper sheets for all of the flowers, apart from the largest petals. If you only have streamers you could leave off the larger petals and make a smaller version.

2 Fold 24in. (60cm) of paper streamer—or a 1¾in. (4.5cm) wide strip of crepe paper the same length—in half lengthwise. The size of the center spiral will depend on the thickness of the crepe. Cut a ½in. (12mm) slit in a straw and, with the folded edge uppermost, slide one end of the crepe paper strip into the slit. Wind a little of the paper into the straw and then wind it around the outside to form the center of the flower.

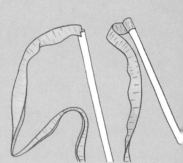

3 Add a little glue on the first couple of spirals only and try to make a domed shape as you wind. Use clear tape to secure and then smear a little glue into the underside of the dome.

4 Choose a different color and measure a length of streamer that will go twice around the center. Fold it in half lengthwise and then over twice widthwise and snip a ⅛in. (3mm) deep frill into the folded edge. Glue around the center coil so the frill stands proud.

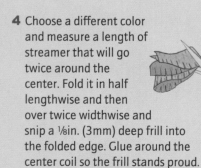

5 Measure the width of the small and large petal templates on page 123. Fold a strip of crepe paper over into four layers so the short ends align with the small template ends. Cut one strip of small petals from the folded paper. Cut two strips of large petals in the same way. Unfold and trim off the two half petals on each end of the small petal strip then glue it around the flower just under the frilled edge.

Crepe paper in yellows, oranges, pink, white, and green

1¾in. (4.5cm) wide crepe paper streamers in yellows, oranges, pink, white, and green

Scissors

Straws

White (PVA) glue

Clear tape

Ruler

Masking tape

6 Glue one large petal strip around the center, butting the base of the petals just below the previous layer.

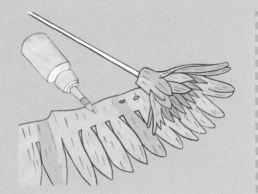

TIP

When cutting the petal strips do not cut through the folded ends of crepe paper at either side of the template—the idea is to achieve one long strip of petals when the strip is unfolded again.

7 Use masking tape to pinch the base together into a cone shape. It will feel a bit squashy and you need to have a balance between making the shape firmer but not pushing it out of shape. Glue on the second large petal strip. Fill in any spaces by cutting individual petals—or several at a time—and gluing them on. Tape the base of the flower again, making sure some of the tape fixes the flower onto the straw.

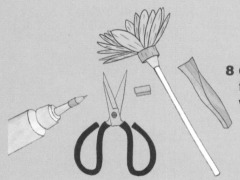

8 Cut two 5in. (12.5cm) long strips of green streamer and fold one twice into a third of its width. Glue it just below where the petals splay out. Trim off any overlap.

9 Using the template on page 123, cut a base strip. Snip 1in. (2.5cm) deep slits at 1in. (2.5cm) intervals along the other edge as marked. Align the zigzag edge a little above where the petals splay out so they are supported a bit more and, as you wind the strip around, overlap the slits so the base of the flower is completely covered with green. Glue the strip in place at intervals.

10 Cut a ¼in. (6mm) wide strip of green and wind it at an angle of 45 degrees around the straw to cover it. Add a dab of glue every now and again. Push any excess strip up into the straw at the bottom.

Patterned
DAFFODILS

Cones use up a lot of paper so this mix-and-match version of daffodil-like flowers gives you flexibility. Make a practice version in white copy paper first—it will look so nice that you might want to stick with plain white. Some of my paper was quite stiff so I used double-stick tape so the cones did not unfurl.

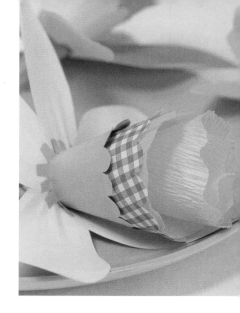

Colored paper in greens and yellows, some with patterns

Scissors

Thin tube or knitting needle

Compass and pencil

White (PVA) glue

Clear tape

Green bendy straws

Crepe paper in yellow and white

Double-stick tape (optional)

1 Using the templates on page 123, for each flower cut five petals, one small trumpet, one large cone, and as many leaves as you want from assorted colored paper.

2 Create soft concertina folds on the bottom third of each petal if your paper is flexible enough—leave flat or make fewer ridges if the paper is too thick. Make a downward pointing valley fold in the center first and work outward. Roll the edges of the petals around a tube to make a soft curve.

3 Draw a 1in. (2.5cm) diameter circle on a piece of paper as a guide. Overlap and glue the edges of the petals around the circle edge so they form a flower with an empty center. Let dry, then remove the flower from the paper.

TIP

When gluing the pieces down to assemble the flower, be sure not to stick them to the paper underneath.

4 Cut the tabs on the small trumpet, then lightly score on the wrong side along the top of the tabs and below the scallops at the top edge. Roll the trumpet into a tube overlapping the last scallop and tab—see the guideline on the template—and glue or tape closed. Fold the tabs out and add a dab of glue to the underside of each. Center the trumpet onto the petals and press down lightly. Let dry. Trim off any petal that shows in the middle hole.

5 Lightly score on the wrong side along the top of the cone below the scallops. Roll into a cone overlapping by one scallop—see guideline on template—and tape or glue closed. Add a small dab of glue halfway down the side and push the cone right down into the small trumpet, lining up the seams.

6 Gently ease the bottom end of a straw down into the flower and out from the point of the cone until the bend plus an extra ½in. (12mm) extends from the bottom of the flower. Secure the small length of straw left inside to the top of the cone with a piece of clear tape.

7 For the inner trumpet cut an 8in. (20cm) square of crepe paper and fold it twice to make a 4in. (10cm) square. Trim the square into a circle and then cut a slit through to the center and cut out a 1in. (2.5cm) diameter center hole. Use your fingers to stretch the outer edge to make as much of a frilly edge as you can.

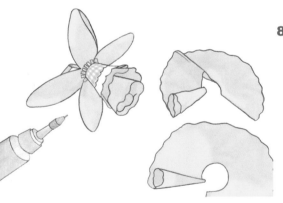

8 Roll one end into a loose cone with a small point and glue down to the main circle along the guideline on the template. The point needs to be small because it will eventually hide the straw in the flower center. Roll the cone over loosely to about one quarter of the way round the main circle and glue down again. Roll the remainder of the shape loosely. Add some dabs of glue into the very bottom of the flower and pop the crepe roll down inside.

TIP

To avoid squashing the crepe paper cone when you glue it, use a knitting needle pushed through the shape to help press the paper together.

9 Roll the bottom of each leaf around a spare straw and glue the overlapping part together, being careful not to glue the leaf to the straw. Remove and let dry. Place one or two leaves onto each flower stalk and push them up the stems as far as you want.

FIERY *Sunflower*

Bring a smile to your face every time you look at this happy open-faced flower. It looks equally good suspended from a ribbon or popped onto a stem and, because it's double sided, it works from every angle. It's easy to scale up or down to fit the space you have by enlarging the central circle and adding more petals—and I feel even happier when I know that I have reused some old scrap paper!

1 For a 14in. (35cm) diameter sunflower, use approximately 24 sheets of scrap paper. Fold each in half lengthwise, open out and fold both sides to the center fold. Fold in half lengthwise again and then in half once more to make a long narrow folded strip.

2 Cut a piece of orange tissue paper measuring 11½ x 2½in. (29 x 6.5cm). Run glue stick down one side of a folded strip and position it, glue down, in the middle of the orange paper. Run glue stick on top of the folded strip and fold over one orange side. Add a bit more glue stick on top and fold in the other edge. Glue in the ends. Cover four strips in one shade of orange.

TIP

Put a thin piece of clear tape (I cut mine in half lengthwise) around the bottom edge of the center spiral to make sure it doesn't unfurl.

3 Roll the strip up into a rough spiral, adding some glue every now and then. Just before you get to the end, add in another strip until you have used all four. Add an elastic band around the outside to keep the roll together while the glue dries.

11 x 8½in. (27.5 x 21.5cm) pieces of scrap white paper

Tissue paper in gold and different shades of orange

Glue stick

Rubber bands

Orange paper

Scissors

White (PVA) glue

Toothpick

Thin orange card

Craft knife and cutting mat

Orange crepe paper

2yd (2m) of ¼in. (6mm) wide orange ribbon

4 Make up approximately ten individual spirals using single folded strips covered in a different shade of orange tissue, using elastic bands and clear tape as before. You may need less or more spirals depending on how thick your paper is. Arrange them around the center to choose the best angle to glue them, and then stick them around the center circle. Let dry. Don't worry if the tissue cracks a little. You can repair it later with small scraps.

5 Make another ten spirals using a third shade of tissue, using the same techniques as before, but this time squash them slightly into a triangular shape. You are aiming to fill in the spaces between the existing small spirals and what will be the edge of the flower center. Glue them in place—there will still be spaces between them.

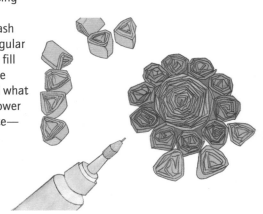

6 Measure the height of the center piece, cut some long orange paper strips to that width and roll them into rough spirals. Squeeze and glue them into the spaces between the triangular shapes to make the flower center as circular in shape as you can.

7 Glue more orange paper strips around the outside of the flower center, overlapping them when necessary. Trim off any excess paper.

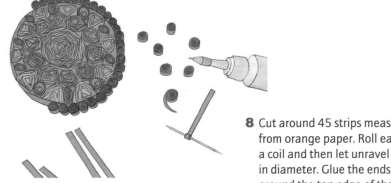

8 Cut around 45 strips measuring 8½ x ¼in. (21.5cm x 6mm) from orange paper. Roll each around a toothpick to make a coil and then let unravel to approximately ½in. (12mm) in diameter. Glue the ends in place and then glue the coils around the top edge of the flower center.

9 Cut two 11 x 2½in. (27.5 x 6.5cm) long strips from thin orange card. Make two score lines to leave a ¼in. (6mm) wide strip down the center and then cut slits at ¾in (18mm) intervals on either side up to the score line. Measure the strips around the outside of the circle and cut off any excess so they butt up to one another neatly.

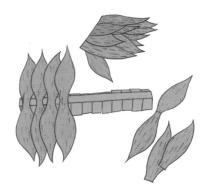

10 Using the double petal template on page 124, cut approximately 44 orange crepe paper double petals, with the grain running from tip to tip as indicated. Use your thumbs to stretch the petals into bowls. Fold the tabs of a card strip so the center strip stands proud. Glue the orange petals along the centre, bowl sides up. You can add as many petals as you can comfortably fit on, just make sure that the cardboard is covered. Make the other strip. Let dry.

TIP

If the crepe paper for the petals is thin, spray glue two sheets together before you start.

11 Turn the card strips over and glue them around the flower center, so they sit on top of the small coil edge made in step 8. Tie the ribbon around the center.

12 Finish the other side by making a second border of coils as in step 8, gluing them around the bottom edge of the flower center.

13 If you want to make your flower fuller, as I did, add another circle of small petals just inside the edge coils—I used about 40 for each side. Cut using the small petal template on page 124 and hold each petal in place with a dab of glue on the base.

Chapter 3
SOPHISTICATED STYLE

Faded
ROSES

There are origami versions of this folding method that are very precise and beautiful but I prefer the quirkiness of casual blooms made with crepe paper. You can make larger roses using a bigger paper strip but a cluster of tiny ones looks fabulous as a wrist corsage. It may take a while to master the technique but it gets easier the more you make.

Watercolors and paintbrushes

White crepe paper

Ruler

Scissors

Plastic sheet or waterproof surface

Absorbent kitchen towel

Toothpicks

White (PVA) glue

Thin wire

Wire cutters

1 Make a strong color first by dipping a paintbrush loaded with color into about three tablespoons of clean water. Test the color out on some spare paper, remembering it will look very different when dry. When you are happy with the strong color, transfer some to a new container and dilute it with more clean water. Then in a third container dilute again to achieve a very pale version.

TIP

Coloring the paper yourself creates a subtle effect—I made my flowers in two different colors, coffee and apricot.

2 For each flower, cut a strip of crepe paper 18 x 3in. (45 x 7.5cm) with the grain vertical to the strip. Lay the strip on a waterproof surface and dampen by brushing all over with clean water. The paper may stretch a little and it will be fragile so take care. Pick up excess water by dabbing with a piece of kitchen towel if necessary.

3 While the strip is still damp, load a paintbrush with the lightest color and paint onto a third of the strip. Painting with the grain is easier.

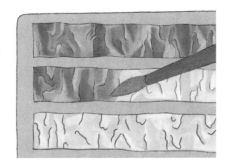

4 Load the paintbrush with the medium color and paint onto the rest. Use the dark color on one end of the strip, which will make the center of the rose. Let dry. If the color is too pale when dry you can dampen the strip again and add more color.

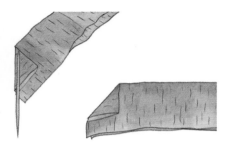

5 Lightly fold the dry strip in half lengthwise; do not make a firm crease because the petal edges should look soft. With the strip fold at the top, turn over one end toward you at 45 degrees and make a light crease so that the lower edge is just over halfway down the folded strip. Turn the strip so the new fold is now vertical and place a toothpick along the 45-degree crease right up to the top point, which will be the center of the rose.

6 Pick the toothpick up in one hand and begin to roll it into the strip. Just as the top gets covered, fold the top of the strip away from the toothpick at an angle with your other hand. Fold it over only a little—the idea is that the top of the strip is still a little higher than the central point of the rose.

7 Continue to roll the strip up the toothpick, folding the strip over and away from you as you go. This does take a little practice but you can unravel and reposition the petals if necessary. Try not to make a triangle shape each time but vary where you make the petal folds.

8 If you are happy with the shape your folds are making, add a dab of glue every now and then to hold them in place. Let dry.

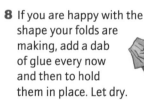

9 Remove the toothpick from the rose and trim the base of the rose at an angle to approximately ½in. (12mm) long. Cut a 6in. (15cm) length of wire, put a dab of glue on the end and insert it into the base of the rose.

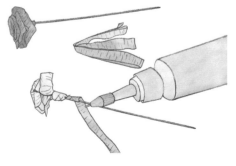

10 Color some crepe paper in a subtle muted green and cut it into strips ¼in. (6mm) wide and approximately 16in. (40cm) long, with the grain vertical to the strip. Glue one end around the back of the rose and wrap the strip around the stem at an angle of 45 degrees, adding a dab of glue every now and then to hold it in place. Let dry and trim off the excess paper.

Dandelion CLOCKS

This is such a versatile method of making a spectacular seed head. I like to make mine with firm, transparent paper to give a delicate, translucent effect and to keep the colors neutral—but it also looks great in bright colors. I'm always surprised at how large the seed head turns out to be.

4in. (10cm) diameter white foam ball

Paintbrush and emulsion paint in a neutral color

Kitchen roll

Thin brown paper

Pencil

Scissors

White (PVA) glue

Double-stick tape

3 kebab sticks

Tracing paper

Ruler

White pencil

Craft knife and cutting mat

Toothpicks

1 Paint the foam ball by dabbing the paint on, removing any excess with a piece of kitchen roll. Let dry.

2 Using the template on page 125, cut four elongated leaf shapes from brown paper. Crumple them up and then flatten out.

3 Glue the leaves one on top of another placed around in a circle. Fold the tips up a little and let dry.

TIP

Pierce a hole in the center of the foliage with the craft knife before pushing the kebab sticks through, so they will go through easier.

4 Attach the foliage onto the ball with double-stick tape so the tips point down. The stem can either be a single kebab stick or, for a thicker stem, glue three kebab sticks together. Push one end of the stem firmly up through the center of the foliage toward the middle of the ball.

5 Cut a 1¾ x 1in. (4.5 x 2.5cm) rectangle from tracing paper. Make a lengthwise fold approximately ¼in. (6mm) wide and press firmly. Open out and place with the fold pointing upward, then color the wider portion downward from the fold to about half the width using white pencil. Use a craft knife or scissors to cut very slender slits along the wide edge, up to the fold.

6 With the fold pointing upward and the frill pointing down, add a smear of glue along the narrow uncut edge of the tracing paper. Position a toothpick at one end so its tip does not go above the frilled edge, and roll it up in the frill. Hold until the glue is dry.

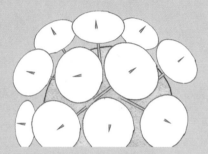

7 Fan out the frill and measure the diameter of the circle it makes. Cut plain circles the same size from scrap paper, push each onto the tip of a toothpick and push the toothpicks into the foam ball to estimate how many seed heads you'll need—I used 120. Space them out so the circles just touch one another and make sure to aim each toothpick at the center of the ball. I find it easier to start at the top and work outward and downward.

8 Remove the toothpicks a few at a time to turn them into finished seeds. To form the seedpod, cut an isosceles triangle 4in. (10cm) long and ½in. (12mm) wide at the base from brown paper. Position the wide end of the triangle at a right angle just where the toothpick end gets fatter, about ¼in. (6mm) from the tip. Add a smear of glue along the paper edge and roll the triangle up tightly, keeping it centered, adding a dab of glue just as you finish rolling. Continue to roll between your fingers until the glue is dry. Make one for each toothpick.

9 Make a frill for each toothpick as explained in steps 4 and 5. It's easier to fan the frill out if you push it well onto a toothpick so the point is visible, which makes it easier to find the center and push out the spokes of the frill. Then add a dab of glue to the point of the toothpick and slide the frill back up to the end so it is level with the point.

10 Replace the finished seeds on the ball, and then begin the next batch. Continue until you have replaced all of the paper circles with seeds. For a smaller dandelion clock, begin with a smaller foam ball and scale down other pieces to match.

Peony WREATH

I worked these pretty peonies up on some foam balls, but you could crumple some paper into a rough ball and tape it to use as a base instead.

White tissue paper

Spray glue

2½in. (6.5cm) and 2in. (5cm) diameter foam balls

Mauve crepe paper

White crepe paper

Scissors

Knitting needle

White (PVA) glue

18-gauge silver colored wire

Wire cutters and round-nosed pliers

Masking tape

Thin stem wire

Dark copper paper (optional)

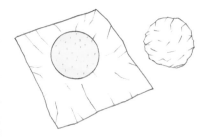

1 For one large mauve flower, cut a 6½in. (16.5cm) square of white tissue paper. Spray glue onto it and cover one of the larger foam balls with it completely.

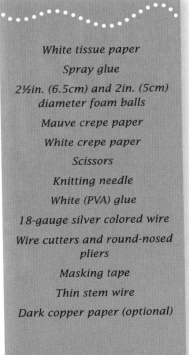

2 Using the templates on page 125 cut out 33 peony petals from the mauve crepe paper, twelve of shape D, six each of shapes B, C, and E and three of shape A. Use your thumbs to tease each petal into a bowl shape. Place the petal onto your fingers and roll the end of a knitting needle across the top edge to frill out the top of the petal.

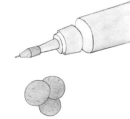

3 Glue the three smallest A circles onto the top of the ball so they overlap in the middle and the grain points towards the center.

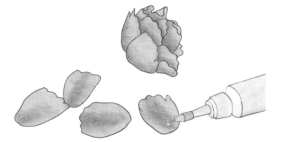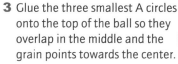

4 Using six B petals, put dabs of glue around the base edge of each petal and glue them around the ball a little further down from the center. Add a circle of C petals, and two circles of D petals, each circle a little further down the ball. Add the final E petal circle and make sure the petals overlap underneath the ball to cover it completely.

5 To make a smaller flower, use a 5in. (12.5cm) square of tissue paper to cover a smaller foam ball, and cut 19 peony petals: three of shape A, six of shape B, and five each of shapes C and D. Glue the petals onto the ball in size order as before.

TIP

Only put glue on a couple of petals at a time as the glue soaks into the paper and dries quickly.

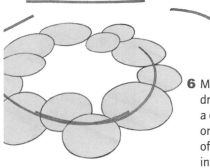

6 My wreath used six large and six smaller flowers. Make one of each size and draw circles in scrap paper to represent them. Arrange the paper circles into a circular wreath design, making sure the center of each larger circle will fall onto the circle of wire that will be the base of the wreath. Cut several lengths of stiff wire varying between 7in. (17.5cm) to 10in. (25cm). Bend the wires into gentle arcs that together will make one complete circle.

TIP

To estimate how long to cut the wires, run each length roughly around the circle between any two large circles. Each large flower should have one wire end nearby.

I bent my wire arcs by hand but you could bend them around a large bucket, the same size as the wreath, if you need to.

7 Work on the large circles first. Take an arc of wire and bend one end up by ¾in. (18mm). Place the spike so it falls in the center of a large paper circle. Make more for adjoining circles, so each large flower will have a spike. Where the wires overlap, secure them together with masking tape. Carry on until you complete the wire circle – mine was 12½in. (31.5cm) in diameter.

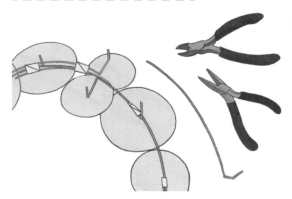

8 Add in more wires for the smaller flowers—these wires will need to bend out at right angles from the wreath circle to reach the center of the paper circle before you make a spike to stand up at the end. The finished circle of wire should have more than one strand all the way around. If it doesn't, just tape on another arc.

9 Make all the flowers you need to complete the wreath, in a mixture of white and mauve.

10 Using the templates on page 125, make three large leaves for the spike of each large flower and a total of 114 smaller leaves for 38 leaf stems (one top and two side leaves for each stem). I used mainly mauve with a few white ones. Curve each leaf into a bowl shape with your thumbs.

11 Cut 38 stem wires, each 6in. (15cm) long, then pinch and glue a small leaf to one end and wind a ¼in. (6mm) wide strip of paper around the stem to hold it in place. Pinch and wind in two small side leaves, adding a dab of glue. Continue to wind the paper down the stem.

12 Wind a ¼in. (6mm) wide strip of crepe paper around the wire circle. Check your design. Add a piece of clear tape to the base of each large leaf to strengthen it, then push three leaves onto each large flower spike. I used mauve for the white flowers and vice versa.

13 Place two leaf stems near each spike. Cut 1in. (2.5cm) rings from a small cardboard tube and place one around each spike. Balance the flowers on top of the tubes to help you visualise the finished result and decide how far out you want the leaves to show.

14 Make a rough sketch or take a reference photo, and then take everything off the wire circle. Starting from the top, work your way around the circle. Wind the leaf stems around the wire circle to secure them and push the flowers down onto their spikes. Make a few more leaf stems if necessary.

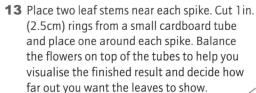

15 An optional step is to make a few more single leaves from a contrasting color, such as a dark copper, using the large leaf template on page 125. Fold each in half lengthwise and then make vein indents with the end of something sharp such as a pin. Glue these leaves individually around the wreath.

Thistle HEADS

You don't need to be able to paint beautifully to achieve interesting color effects for these specimens, which remind me of something halfway between a thistle and an artichoke. It's very striking if you make some smaller versions as well as the larger ones, to give a sense of scale.

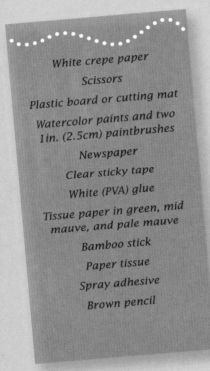

White crepe paper

Scissors

Plastic board or cutting mat

Watercolor paints and two 1in. (2.5cm) paintbrushes

Newspaper

Clear sticky tape

White (PVA) glue

Tissue paper in green, mid mauve, and pale mauve

Bamboo stick

Paper tissue

Spray adhesive

Brown pencil

1 For a large thistle, cut nine strips of white crepe paper each 15 x 2¾in. (37.5 x 7cm), with the grain vertical to the strip. Lay the strips out on a plastic board.

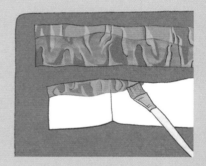

2 Mix two colors, pink and green. Put a couple of tablespoons of water in a palette, swirl a wet paintbrush in the pink and dilute the color by dipping the paintbrush into the water. Check it's the right density on a piece of scrap paper, then swirl the pink onto the top third of the strip. Quickly change to green and stroke it over the rest of the strip. Let dry. Check the paint has penetrated through the paper so you have color on both sides—add a little more color if you need to.

3 Fold the pink and green strip until it is the right size to draw a scale on, using the scale template on page 126. With the pink at the top cut out several scales at once—I used 73 scales for the large thistle but you may need fewer or more. Use your thumbs to mold the center of all the scales into a cupped shape.

4 Crumple some newspaper into a small ball that is firm enough to hold its shape but not rock solid. Wind sticky tape around it to hold the shape. Add more crumpled paper, taping it here and there to support the shape, until you have the size you want. For the large thistle, I made my ball approximately 5in. (12.5cm) in diameter.

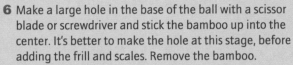

5 Cover the ball with a thin layer of papier-mâché by tearing some newspaper into small pieces and sticking them round the outside with a little watered-down glue. Cover the ball with a sheet of green tissue paper that is a similar color to the scales. Let dry.

6 Make a large hole in the base of the ball with a scissor blade or screwdriver and stick the bamboo up into the center. It's better to make the hole at this stage, before adding the frill and scales. Remove the bamboo.

7 For the inner frill, cut one strip 4 x 20in. (10 x 50cm) in each of the two mauve color tissues. Cut a 1 x 20in. (2.5 x 50cm) strip of crepe paper, with grain vertical to the strip, and glue it onto one of the mauve strips ¼in. (6mm) up from one edge. Add the second mauve strip on top, gluing it to the crepe paper.

8 Fold all layers of the strip over in half, then over again. Cut out some slender triangles along the unglued edge about 2in. (5cm) deep. Below the crepe paper along the other edge make little snips ¼in. (6mm) deep to create tabs about ¼in. (6mm) wide.

9 For the middle frill, cut four strips 3½ x 20in. (9 x 50cm) from the pale mauve tissue. Layer two strips on the bottom, add the crepe paper as in step 7 then add the second two strips of tissue on top. Prepare both edges as in step 8.

10 For the outer frill, cut two strips 3 x 20in. (7.5 x 50cm) from the pale mauve tissue. Add the crepe paper and prepare both edges as in steps 7–8, but this time cut the crepe paper only ½in. (12mm) wide.

11 Make one more frill by cutting two strips of 2 x 20in. (5 x 50cm) from pale mauve tissue. Don't use crepe on this frill and cut the slender triangles only 1in. (2.5cm) deep.

12 Starting at the very top of the thistle with the inner frill, fold out the tabs and glue them onto the thistle as you wind the frill around. Leave a little space between each spiral. Carry on adding the other frills in order in the same way.

13 Tear a soft paper tissue into little pieces and make a little pad to fit in the middle of each scale to plump it out. Put glue around the scale edge but leave the top quarter without glue. Glue one scale at a time around the top of the globe so they cover the bottom edge of the frill. Press around the edges and try not to flatten the centers. Continue to add scales, overlapping them and gluing them between one another until the whole globe is covered. Let dry.

14 Cut a long strip of green tissue paper, a textured one if you have some, and spray some adhesive lightly onto it. Wrap it around the bamboo tightly, leaving a small length of bamboo uncovered at the top. Push any extra tissue up into the bamboo at the bottom.

15 Stick two sheets of crepe paper together with spray adhesive and paint them green on both sides. Let dry. Cut out two stem leaf shapes and six thistle head leaf shapes using the templates on page 126. Draw a brown pencil line down the center of each leaf.

16 Wrap and glue the two stem leaves a few inches down from the top of the bamboo. Glue the thistle head leaves around the base of the flower. Squeeze some glue into the hole in the base you made in step 6 and push the tip of bamboo up into it.

17 Spread out the frills a little more and cut more slits down the frills between the scales if necessary.

SMALL THISTLE VARIATION

Follow the steps for the large thistle, but use the scale template on page 126 reduced by 80% and the thistle head leaf reduced by 60%. I used 50 scales for my small thistle. In step 4 make a 3½in. (9cm) diameter ball. Omit the frills in steps 7–12 and instead glue the scales right up to the top of the flower. Since the smaller thistle has a shorter stem I didn't add stem leaves.

Dogtooth VIOLETS

These droop beautifully and are delicate little things, but you need to find some paper with the right sort of "bend." Colored copy paper is good and I prefer to use paper with a color on both sides. They do use a lot of paper for such a little flower, so take time to plan out your template pattern first.

Colored paper
Pencil
Scissors
Pin
Thin tube or knitting needle
White (PVA) glue
Yellow tissue paper
Ruler
Toothpick
Gold wire and wire cutters
Round-nosed pliers
Stem wire
Large tube

1 For each flower, cut a flower shape using the template on page 126. Pierce a hole in the middle as marked. Roll the petals lengthwise around a thin tube to give them a slight curve. Put a little glue onto each small triangle around the center and overlap the base of each petal over the triangle on the base of the next petal.

2 Roll each petal around the thin tube the other way to curve the tip of the petal out and down.

3 Cut a 3 x 1½in. (7.5 x 4cm) rectangle from yellow tissue for each flower. Fold it in half widthwise to make a square and cut a delicate frill three quarters of the way down the edge opposite the fold. Roll the intact edge around a toothpick, using a dab of glue every now and then. Keep the layers on top of one another as much as you can. Remove from the toothpick and let dry.

4 Cut a 4in. (10cm) piece of gold wire for each flower. Fold in half and use round-nosed pliers to make a little ring at each end, facing away from one another.

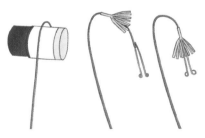

5 Cut a stem wire and bend one end around a large tube to make a curve, then bend the very end into a small loop. Push the frill onto the curve with the fronds facing toward the end. Hook the loop on the end of the stem around the middle of the gold wire and then squeeze it together to hold the gold wire firmly. Pull the frill down to hide the join.

6 Enlarge the hole in the middle of the flower so it is large enough for the wire. Push the bottom of the stem into the bowl of the flower and slide the flower up around the curve. Put a little dab of glue around the top of the frill just before you slide the flower down onto it.

ELEGANT *Lilies*

Make some plain versions of these lilies first as practice stems before you experiment with color. The paper has to have some degree of "give" to it, and crepe paper was by far the best thing I found.

Crepe paper

Scissors

Water-soluble felt tip pens

Thin white string

White (PVA) glue

Colored paper

10in. (25cm) straws

Clear tape

Kitchen paper

1 Cut a lily petal shape from white crepe paper using the template on page 124. Using a water-soluble felt tip, lightly color a ³⁄₁₆in. (4mm) thick line ³⁄₁₆in. (4mm) in from the petal edge all round the sides and tip, leaving the bottom edge uncolored. Turn the petal over and go over the line again on the other side. With the highest bulge of the shape to the left, lightly brush some pale green on the bottom third of the petal on one side only.

2 Run a very thin line of glue right around the sides and tip of the petal. Starting at the top and leaving an end of 1in. (5cm), stick a length of string all down the right edge. Butt a second length of string up to the one in place at the top, then stick down the left side. Let dry.

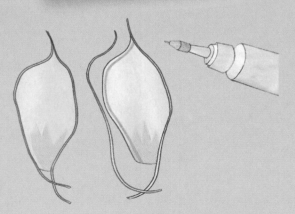

3 Put a line of glue along the top of each length of string and then roll the colored edge of the petal over the string to make a thicker defined edge to the petal. Let dry.

TIP

The rolled edge will be the back of the petal. If you are making a bunch of these, it's easier to make a good arrangement if some of the flowers are made as a mirror image.

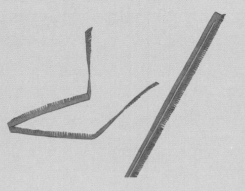

4 Cut several ½in. (12mm) x 12in. (30cm) strips of colored paper. Fold each strip over twice to make four layers and cut a fine fringe ¼in. (6mm) deep all along one long edge. Open out flat and curl each strip along a knitting needle lengthwise.

5 Cut a small slit at the top of the straw and insert the end of a strip, with the frill uppermost and curving outward. Wind the strip down the straw at an angle so that the frill stands proud. Add a little glue every now and then to keep the frill in place and stop when it covers 6in. (15cm) of the straw. Add on a new strip when you need to—I wound my frill so it was quite irregular. Glue the end down.

6 Tape a second straw onto the bottom of the first. Cut several ¼in. (6mm) wide strips of paper in the same color as the frill. Glue the end of one onto the bottom of the frill and wind it around the straw at an angle of 45 degrees. Butt the paper up on each wind to make a smooth surface and add a dab of glue every now and then to keep it in place. Add on new strips until both straws are completely covered.

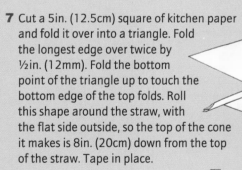

7 Cut a 5in. (12.5cm) square of kitchen paper and fold it over into a triangle. Fold the longest edge over twice by ½in. (12mm). Fold the bottom point of the triangle up to touch the bottom edge of the top folds. Roll this shape around the straw, with the flat side outside, so the top of the cone it makes is 8in. (20cm) down from the top of the straw. Tape in place.

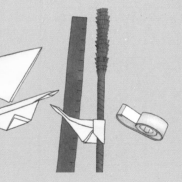

8 Turn the petal over so the rolled edge is underneath and use your thumbs to stretch the middle into more of a bowl shape. Cut several small triangles out of the bottom edge. Trim off the excess string at top and bottom.

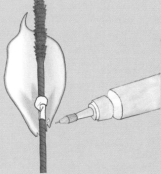

9 Place the straw on top of the petal so the bottom of the cone is approximately ½in. (12mm) up from the base of the petal. Add a little glue on the inside edge of the bottom 2in. (5cm) of the right side of the petal and roll it over the cone to the left. Smear a little glue on the inside edge of the bottom 2in. (5cm) of the left side of the petal and roll it over to the right.

Musical ROSES

You can make these flowers as full as you want simply by adding more petals; it just depends on how much paper you have. I am not advocating cutting up intact sheet music—use old tattered pages or make black and white copies and use those instead.

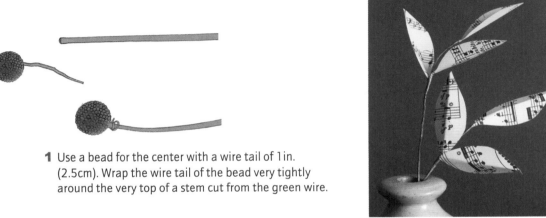

1 Use a bead for the center with a wire tail of 1in. (2.5cm). Wrap the wire tail of the bead very tightly around the very top of a stem cut from the green wire.

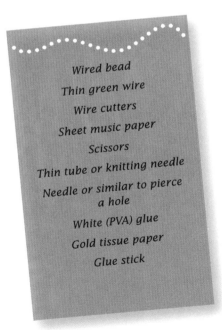

Wired bead

Thin green wire

Wire cutters

Sheet music paper

Scissors

Thin tube or knitting needle

Needle or similar to pierce a hole

White (PVA) glue

Gold tissue paper

Glue stick

TIP

My wire-tail beads were from a craft store but you could easily make them yourself by gluing a short length of wire into the hole of any bead.

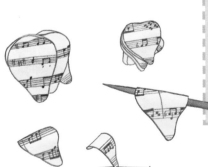

2 Cut out the petals using the templates on page 121; for each flower, you will need three small, six medium, and seven large petals. Curl the wider end of each petal away from you around a thin tube such as a knitting needle. Pierce a hole in the base of each petal—use something the same size as the wire.

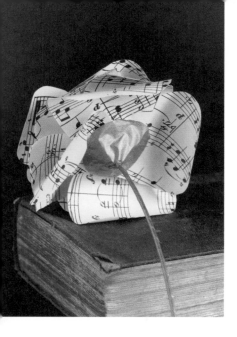

3 Slide each petal, starting with the smallest and with the curve pointing downward, up the stem. Just below the center bead add some glue around the base of the petal and pinch it tightly around the stem. Hold until the glue sets. Arrange the small petals overlapping each other a little.

4 Join the medium petals on in the same way and then the largest petals. Let dry. If the paper is quite stiff, cut a couple of tiny slits near the base of the petal to help ease it around the wire.

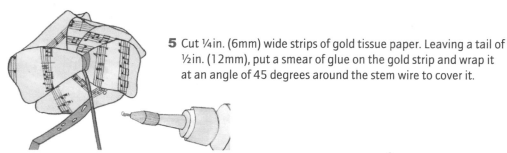

5 Cut ¼in. (6mm) wide strips of gold tissue paper. Leaving a tail of ½in. (12mm), put a smear of glue on the gold strip and wrap it at an angle of 45 degrees around the stem wire to cover it.

6 Cut a 1½in. (4cm) diameter circle of gold tissue, make a slit into the center and slide the wire into the slit. Use a glue stick to stick the circle to the back of the flower to neaten it up.

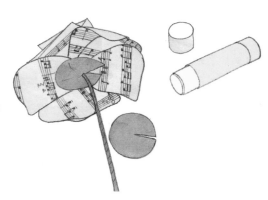

7 Cut out some leaves using the top leaf template on page 125 and crease each in half. Place the bottom of one leaf under the end of a short length of wire—I used a slightly thinner wire than the stem wire because it was more flexible. Leaving a tail of ½in. (12mm), put a smear of glue on another gold strip and wrap it at an angle of 45 degrees around the wire and the leaf. Cover the wire for 1½in. (4cm) and wrap in one side leaf, and then the other. Continue down to the bottom of the wire.

Valentine
FLOWER

This flower is a real labor of love and I won't deny it is a bit fiddly to create—but it's well worth the effort. I have made a floaty, feminine very pale pink flower but you could make an outrageous version in bright cyclamen and hot pinks. The finished flower is approximately 16in. (40cm) in diameter.

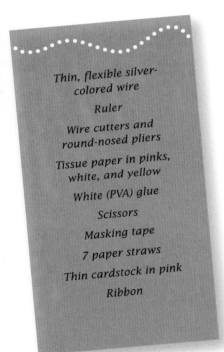

Thin, flexible silver-colored wire

Ruler

Wire cutters and round-nosed pliers

Tissue paper in pinks, white, and yellow

White (PVA) glue

Scissors

Masking tape

7 paper straws

Thin cardstock in pink

Ribbon

1 Cut the wire for 15 wire hearts, five of each size; small hearts use 19in. (48cm) of wire, medium ones use 23in. (58cm), and large ones use 26in. (66cm). Using the pliers, bend 2in. (5cm) at each end into a right angle facing outward.

2 Bend each length of wire round and twist the right angle ends together so you have a circular shape with a "stalk" at the bottom. Push the center top of the circle down with your finger to make a deep indent. Squeeze the indent smaller with pliers and mold the wire into a soft curving heart shape with your fingers.

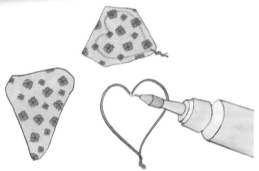

3 Make up all the wire hearts. Cut out pieces of tissue paper a little larger than the hearts—I used patterned pink for the small hearts, white for the medium hearts and plain pink for the large hearts. Smear glue around the wire and place the paper gently on top of it, smoothing it gently down over the wire. Let dry.

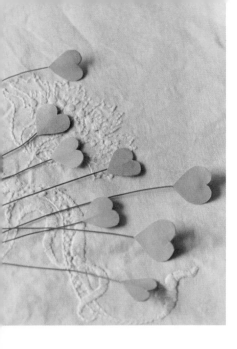

4 Trim off the excess paper around the wire. Don't worry if the wire separates from the paper a little—simply glue it back on.

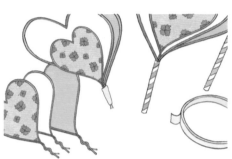

5 Arrange the petals in sets of three, one of each size, and wrap some masking tape around the twisted metal stalks. Cut 5in. (12.5cm) lengths of straw and push the stalk of a set of three petals into the top of each straw.

6 Cut a 4 x 9in. (10 x 23cm) strip of yellow tissue paper and fold it in half lengthwise. Then fold in half widthwise and cut slits along the top folded edge to halfway down. Open out the widthwise fold so you have a 9in. (23cm) long frill.

7 Position one end of the frill under the top 1in. (2.5cm) of another length of straw, with the frill pointing up. Roll the straw up in the frill, adding a little glue every now and again.

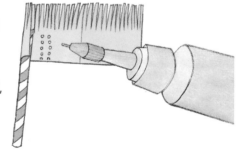

8 Group all the petal straws around the frilled straw. You may have to add an empty straw, as I did, to make sure the frilled straw will be in the center. Hold the straws in place temporarily with an elastic band before wrapping a strip of masking tape around to hold them permanently.

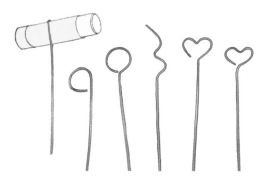

9 Cut some 7in. (17.5cm) lengths of wire. Wrap one end of each around a ¾in. (18mm) diameter tube to make a circle. Remove from the tube and pull the circle until it is centered over the wire. Shape the circle to mold it into a heart shape. Make a curve in the tail of the wire.

10 Make as many heart wires as you want, tape the ends together, and carefully push them down into the middle of the frilled center. Rearrange the hearts to make a pretty pattern.

11 Cut several heart small shapes in pairs from the pink cardstock using the template on page 127. Cut more wires in several different lengths of around 7in. (17.5cm). Tape the top of a wire to the back of a heart with a small piece of masking tape. Glue a matching heart on top to cover the wire end completely.

12 Make several pink hearts and push the wires into the frilled center of the flower again. Finish the main stem of the flower by wrapping a ribbon around it to cover the straws.

Climbing VINE

These are made from clear cellophane—I used some with a lovely polka dot pattern. You can turn them into any color you want just by changing the lining; tissue paper makes the best liner because you need something that is very thin and flexible. I like to make several long vine strands with flowers shooting out on alternate sides and mini florets on twisty stems.

Cellophane wrap, preferably with a pattern

Tissue paper in blues and greens

Scissors

Stem wire

Clear tape

Green raffia ribbon

White (PVA) glue

Long length of wire

1 To make one floret, cut a 5½in. (14cm) square of cellophane and place a 3½in. (9cm) diameter tissue paper circle in the middle. Fold over into a triangle, position the end of a 4in. (10cm) length of wire just above the middle of the folded edge and fix in place with a tiny piece of clear tape. With the middle of the folded edge as the central point, fold one third of the triangle over the wire toward you and the other third away from you. Then fold in half again to make a very narrow triangle. Place a thin piece of tape around the point to keep it closed.

2 Open out the raffia ribbon and glue one end around the base of the floret. Wind the raffia around the wire at an angle of 45 degrees, adding a dab of glue every now and then. If your raffia is very wide, cut it in half. I rather like it if the result is a little lumpy. Trim off the ends.

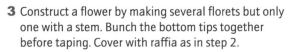

3 Construct a flower by making several florets but only one with a stem. Bunch the bottom tips together before taping. Cover with raffia as in step 2.

TIP

Make lots of individual florets, keep some single, and group the rest together in different numbers, depending on how large you want to make the flowers. Alter the length of the stems as well.

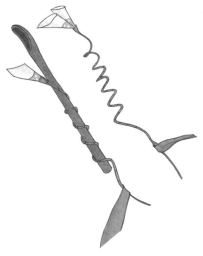

4 Make a smaller floret using a 3½in. (9cm) diameter cellophane circle and a 2in. (5cm) circle of tissue paper. It's the same technique as in step 1 but wind the wire stem around a large tube when you've made it so that it's nice and twisty.

5 Wrap a length of wire with raffia as before, place it on a surface, bend the vine strand into a nice shape and arrange your flowers along it. Take some extra raffia, open it out, put some dabs of glue on it and wrap it around the ends of the flower wires to attach them to the vine.

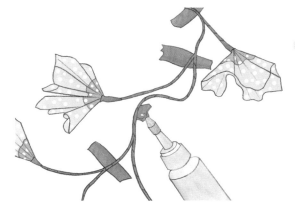

Honesty SEEDHEADS

A huge bunch of these seedheads looks impressive, but one or two sprays in a vase look even better because you can see the structure properly. I like to make them larger than life for maximum effect. Sometimes the edges of the pods separate a little but then so do the edges of real ones.

Thick and thinner gauges of silver-colored wire

Ruler

Wire cutters

Wide masking tape

Dried pulses

Black felt-tip pen

6½in. (16.5cm) diameter tube

Flat-nosed pliers

Tracing paper

Scissors

Pencil

White (PVA) glue

Spray adhesive

One-part epoxy contact adhesive

Silver tissue paper

1 Each stem has 5–7 pods. Cut one 18in. (45cm) length of thicker wire for the stem and some 9½in. (24cm) lengths of thinner wire for the pods.

2 Fold over the ends of a length of masking tape and tape it sticky side up on a work surface. Put some pulses onto the tape and color them with the black pen. When dry, turn them over and color the other side. Let dry.

3 Wrap the end of one of the lengths of thin wire around the tube, overlapping the ends by ½in. (12mm) and then twisting the end back around the wire to make a circle on a stalk. Remove from the tube and squeeze the top end of the circle with the pliers to make a small point. Use your fingers to make the circle into more of an oval shape. Repeat with the other lengths of thin wire.

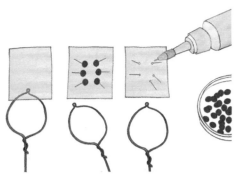

4 Cut two pieces of tracing paper for each wire oval, both larger than the oval. Place a wire oval on one piece and use it as a guide to draw several ½in. (12mm) long thin black spokes in pencil from the edge toward the middle. Remove the wire. Add a tiny dab of PVA glue at the inner end of each spoke and position a seed on top—the seeds need to be far enough away from the edge of the pod so the two layers of tracing paper will touch beyond them and stay sealed. Repeat for each wire oval.

5 Spray the seeded papers, the wire ovals, and the unseeded papers with adhesive. Add another tiny dab of white (PVA) glue to the top of each seed. Place each wire oval onto a seeded paper then cover with a piece of unseeded paper and press firmly together. Let dry.

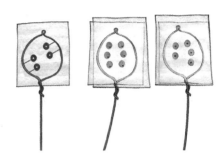

6 Trim the excess paper as close to the wire as you can. Place your thumbnail over the wire at the very ends to help tear off any extra paper because the scissors can't reach there.

7 Make a gentle curve in the stem wire, place it on the work surface and lay the pods down where you want them to fall on each side, curving the stalk of each away from the stem. Trim off any excess stalk.

8 Attach the stalks to the stem wire with a little of the contact adhesive. I dip the end of a stalk a little way into the tube and then balance the stalk on top of the stem so they are touching for the last 1in. (2.5cm) or so. Let dry.

9 Wrap a ¼in. (6mm) strip of silver tissue paper around the joins to neaten them, using a smear of white (PVA) glue to stick the tissue in place.

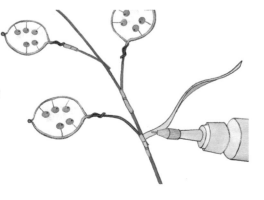

CHERRY *Blossom*

My vision of cherry blossom is always a cluster of pale pink clouds amongst dark branches, so you could try to find a suitable branch to attach the blossom onto. I discovered a thick wire with dark string wound around it and decided to make a small circlet to decorate with the delicate blossom.

String-covered wire and wire cutters

White crepe paper

Scissors

Pin

Water-soluble felt-tip pens in pinks

Plastic board or waterproof mat

Water and paintbrush

Kitchen roll

Colored pencil in pink

Thin silver wire

Seed beads in dark red

White (PVA) glue

Dark red crepe paper

Clear tape

Round-nose pliers

1 Overlap the end of the wire to form a 10in. (25cm) diameter circle, twist the end around the circle to secure and then cut off leaving a little of the end standing out. Add another couple of lengths of wire so you have several ends sticking out at intervals around the circle.

TIP

If you can't find string-covered wire like mine you could cover plain wire by winding around string or strips of brown tissue paper.

2 I made 24 flowers for my circle because I wanted to leave some of it bare. Cut out the flowers several at a time from white crepe paper using the template on page 127. Push a pin through the center of each. Make more than you think you will need in case the coloring isn't always to your liking.

3 Draw a circle in the middle of each flower with a felt-tip pen leaving a clear area in the center ⅜in. (9mm) in diameter. Make some circles with a thicker line than others. Drop some clean water from a paintbrush onto the empty center and watch how the color moves away from it into the petals. Add the water a little at a time to get the effect you want. Let dry completely.

4 Now is the time for experimentation. Draw on some colored dots with a darker pink felt-tip and add thin radiating lines with a colored pencil.

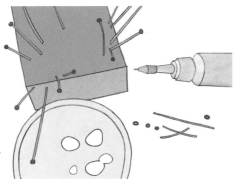

5 For each flower, cut four 1½in. (4cm) lengths and one longer—at least 4in. (10cm)—length of wire. The longer wire will wrap around the basic frame. Dip one end of each wire into the glue and then pop it into a seed bead. Let dry.

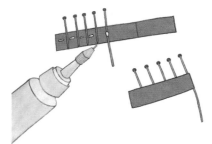

6 Cut a ¾in. (18mm) wide by 5½in. (14cm) long strip of dark red crepe paper for each flower. Glue the five wires at intervals along one half so the beads are at the same level and the shorter wires are level with the bottom of the strip. Smear some glue across the wires to halfway along the paper and then fold the other half over the top.

7 Roll the crepe paper up into a tube, adding a dab of glue now and again. Cut a ¼in. (6mm) wide strip of dark red crepe paper, smear it with glue and wind it tightly around the bottom of the tube, then continue wrapping down the long wire at an angle of 45 degrees. Add some glue at intervals to secure.

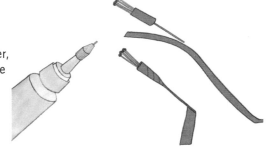

8 Overlap the petals of the flowers a little and glue the edges to make each flower into a nice open bowl shape. Use the pin to enlarge the center hole a little more if necessary and push the long wire through until the flower sits halfway up the paper roll. Add a dab of glue to the underside of the flower to attach it more securely to the roll. Splay out the wires a little. You can tidy up the underneath with red felt-tip pen if you want a super neat result.

9 Use masking tape and more crepe paper strips to bind some of the flowers into clusters of three. Wind the long wires of each flower or set of flowers into the wire circle to make clusters of flowers at intervals around.

EXOTIC *Orchids*

These are made from just three basic shapes and they use only a small amount of paper so you can afford to use one of your special pieces. You may not be able to get the same silver patterned paper I used, but they also work well in plain paper.

Patterned paper in silver and grey

Mauve paper

Scissors

Thin tube or knitting needle

Pin

Sponge (optional)

Mauve wire and wire cutters

Round-nosed pliers

Large mauve and smaller silver seed beads

White (PVA) glue

Silver colored wire

Clear tape

Mauve tissue paper

1 For each flower cut out three petal shapes in assorted papers using the templates on page 127. Roll the petal edges around a thin tube to make soft curves. Group the petals in sets of three and pierce a hole through the center of all three with a pin—it might be easier to use a sponge as a base if the paper is thick.

TIP
Some patterned paper can make it difficult to see the structure of the flower properly, so it helps if you use plain paper for some layers. And it's worth the effort to space the layers apart with seed beads, as long as you make sure the wire will go through them before you begin.

2 Cut a 5in. (12.5cm) length of mauve wire and make a small loop at one end with the round-nosed pliers. Thread on one mauve bead, the smallest petal shape, two silver beads, the middle petal shape, two silver beads, the largest petal shape, two silver beads, and the final mauve bead. Add a dab of glue to each bead as you position it.

3 Make two more flowers, one with a longer stem of approximately 9in. (22.5cm).

4 Cut a bud petal for each of three buds using the template on page 127. Curl the edges over a thin tube as before and pierce a hole in the middle with a pin. Cut a 3in. (7.5cm) length of mauve wire and make a small loop at one end. Thread on a mauve bead, the bud petal, two silver beads and one more mauve bead. Add a dab of glue on every bead as you position them.

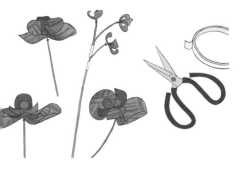

5 Cut a long silver stem wire. Using a very slim piece of masking tape wrap the stem of one bud around the top of the silver wire stem. Add on the two other buds, alternating them left and right on the stem. Tape on the three flowers, alternating them as well, ending with the one with the longest stem.

6 Cut some ¼in. (6mm) wide strips of mauve tissue paper and wrap them at an angle of 45 degrees around the stem wires to cover up all tape and silver wire.

Templates

The following templates are either used at the size they appear here or should be enlarged to 200% on a photocopier, as noted on each template. If an arrow appears by the side of the template, this shows the direction of the "grain" when using crepe paper. Fine dotted lines indicate scoring lines, rather than cutting lines.

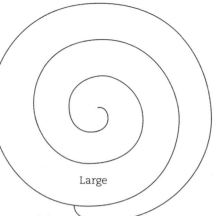

Small

Spiral Ranunculus
(see page 10)
Topiary Cone
(see page 60)
Photocopy at 200%

Large

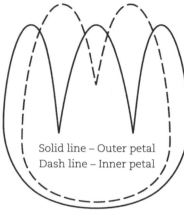

Solid line – Outer petal
Dash line – Inner petal

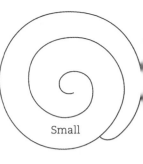

Alternative flower designs

Graphic Tulips
(see page 16)
Use at this size

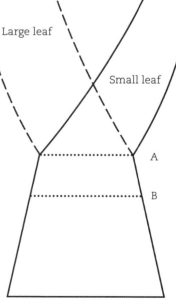

Large leaf

Small leaf

A

B

Seed Packets
(see page 24)
Photocopy at 200%

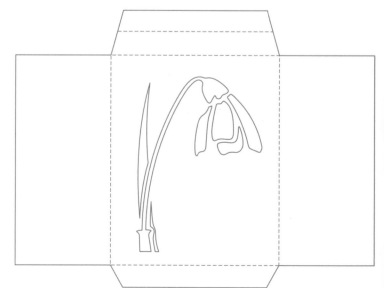

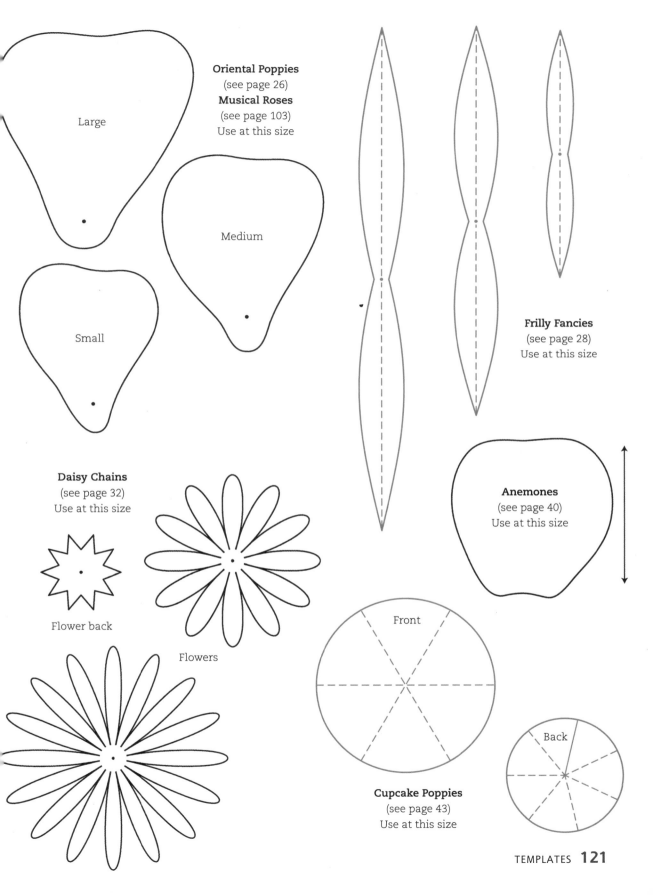

Large

Oriental Poppies
(see page 26)
Musical Roses
(see page 103)
Use at this size

Medium

Small

Frilly Fancies
(see page 28)
Use at this size

Daisy Chains
(see page 32)
Use at this size

Anemones
(see page 40)
Use at this size

Flower back

Flowers

Front

Back

Cupcake Poppies
(see page 43)
Use at this size

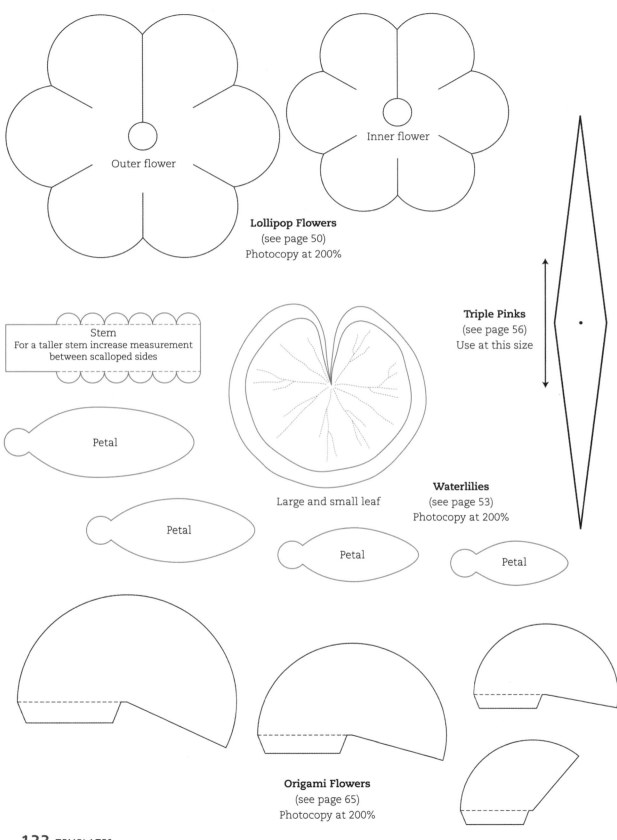

Outer flower

Inner flower

Lollipop Flowers
(see page 50)
Photocopy at 200%

Stem
For a taller stem increase measurement
between scalloped sides

Petal

Petal

Petal

Petal

Large and small leaf

Triple Pinks
(see page 56)
Use at this size

Waterlilies
(see page 53)
Photocopy at 200%

Origami Flowers
(see page 65)
Photocopy at 200%

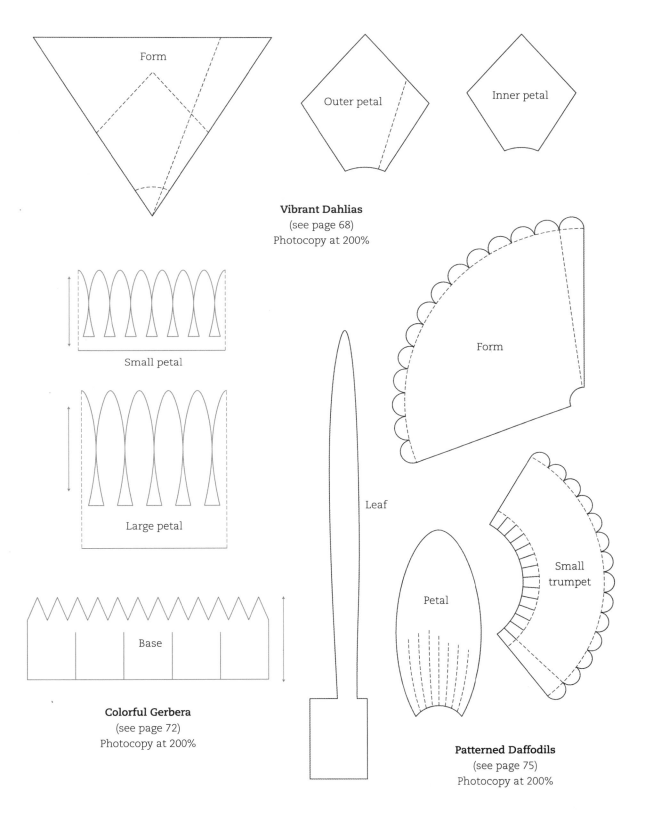

Form

Outer petal

Inner petal

Vibrant Dahlias
(see page 68)
Photocopy at 200%

Small petal

Large petal

Base

Form

Leaf

Petal

Small trumpet

Colorful Gerbera
(see page 72)
Photocopy at 200%

Patterned Daffodils
(see page 75)
Photocopy at 200%

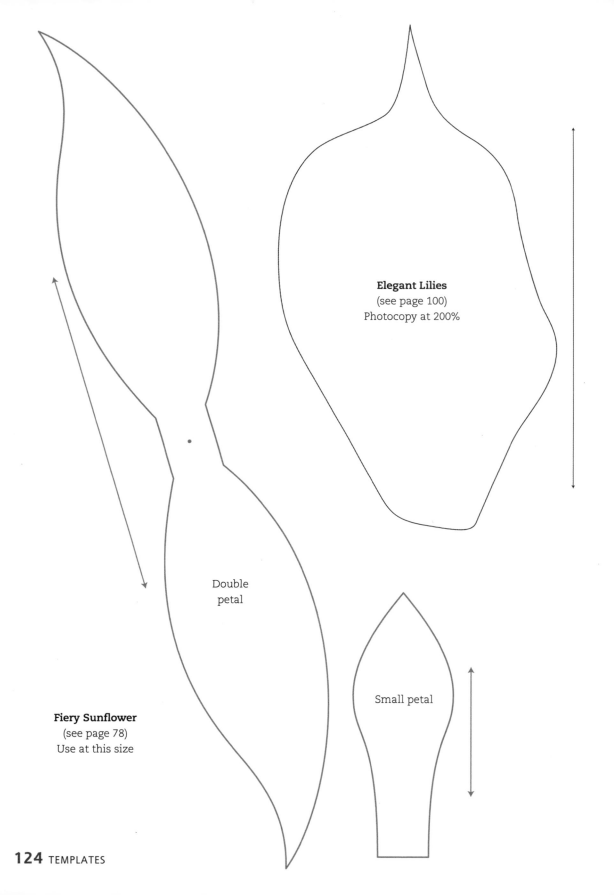

Elegant Lilies
(see page 100)
Photocopy at 200%

Double
petal

Small petal

Fiery Sunflower
(see page 78)
Use at this size

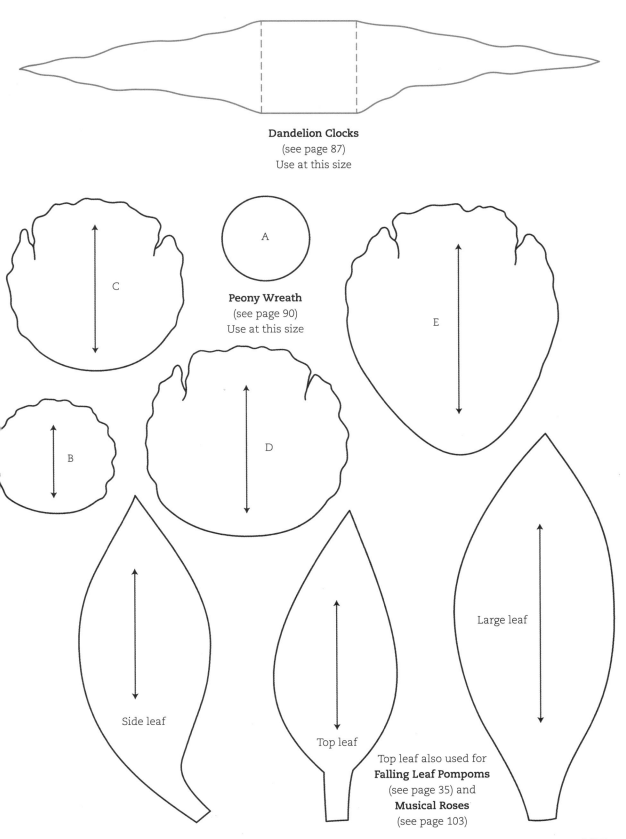

Dandelion Clocks
(see page 87)
Use at this size

A

C

Peony Wreath
(see page 90)
Use at this size

E

B

D

Side leaf

Top leaf

Large leaf

Top leaf also used for
Falling Leaf Pompoms
(see page 35) and
Musical Roses
(see page 103)

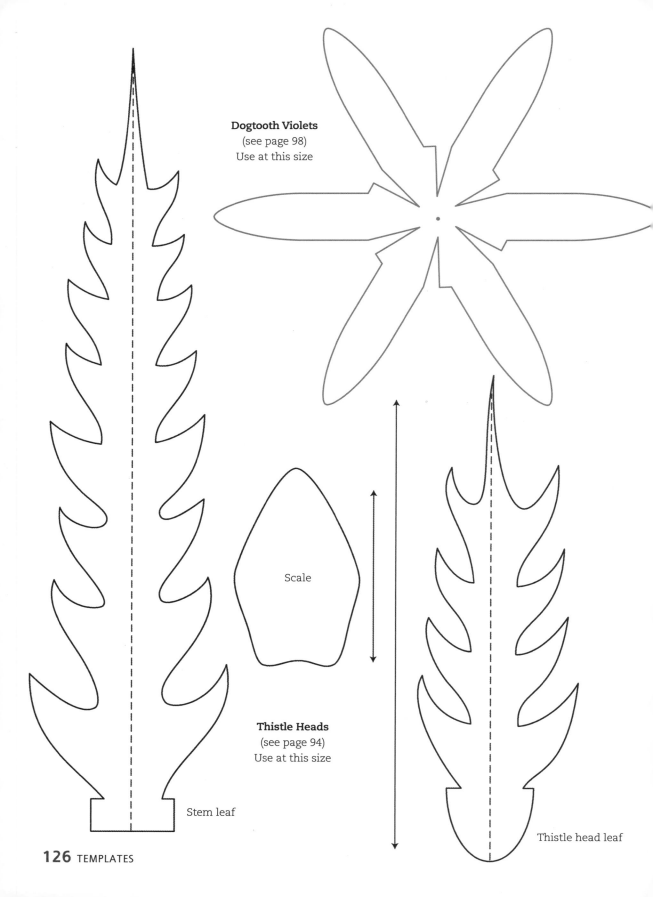

Dogtooth Violets
(see page 98)
Use at this size

Scale

Thistle Heads
(see page 94)
Use at this size

Stem leaf

Thistle head leaf

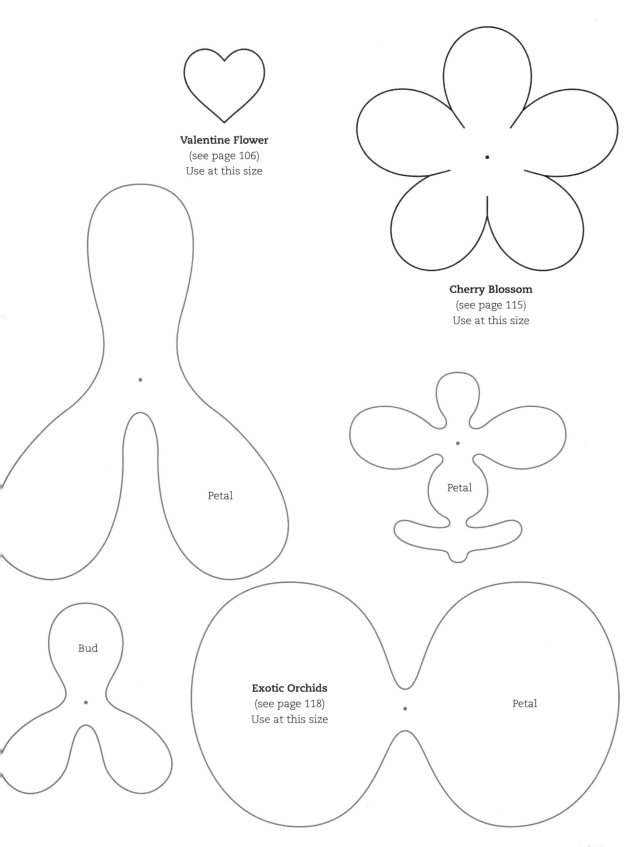

Valentine Flower
(see page 106)
Use at this size

Cherry Blossom
(see page 115)
Use at this size

Petal

Petal

Bud

Exotic Orchids
(see page 118)
Use at this size

Petal

Resources and index

I like to recycle papers and use scraps in my projects, but have also found the following sources useful:

US

Artist & Craftsman
www.artistcraftsman.com

Dollar Tree
www.dollartree.com

Hobby Lobby
www.hobbylobby.com

Home Depot
www.homedepot.com

Kelly Paper
www.kellypaper.com

Michaels.com
Michaels.com

Northwest Art & Frame
4733 California Ave SW
Seattle WA 98116

Quilling Superstore
www.quillingsuperstore.com

UK

Hobbycraft
www.hobbycraft.co.uk

Paperchase
www.paperchase.co.uk

Shepherds Falkiners
www.falkiners.com

Author's Acknowledgments

Once again, a huge thank you to the team at Cico for working so hard on my book—Cindy Richards, Sally Powell, Gillian Haslam, Fahema Khanam, Geoff Borin, Jo Henderson, and Nel Haynes— and especially my editor, Marie Clayton.

A
anemones 40–42
arranging flowers 6

C
cactus lights, flowering 46–49
catkins, spray of 13–15
cherry blossom 115–117
chives 30–31
chrysanthemums 21–23
color 6
cones, topiary 60–61
containers, rice 6, 27

D
daffodils, patterned 75–77
dahlias, vibrant 68–71
daisy chains 32–34
dandelion clocks 87–89

E
equipment 6

F
flat flowers 16–17
freestanding flowers 16–17
frilly fancies 28–31

G
garlands 19, 32, 115
gerbera, colorful 72–74
glue 6
grape hyacinths 62–64

H
honesty seedheads 112–114

L
leaves, making 6
lights, cactus 46–49
lilies, elegant 100–102
lollipop flowers 50–52
loopy flowers 18–20

N
napkins 6, 36, 40–43

O
orchids, exotic 118–119
origami flowers 65–67
oriental poppies 26–27

P
paper 6
   cellophane 110

coffee filters 6, 57
crepe 6, 30, 40, 57, 73, 77, 84, 91, 94, 100, 115
cupcake liners 43
double-sided 6, 16, 49, 50, 65, 98
envelopes 6, 21
giftwrap 6, 50
magazines 21–23
napkins 6, 36
quilling 18, 49, 63
sheet music 103–105
strips 18–20
tissue 26, 29, 35, 41, 46, 65, 69, 79, 91, 94, 98, 106, 110
tracing 53, 87, 112
peony wreath 90–93
pinks, triple 56–59
pompoms, falling leaf 35–37
poppies
   cupcake 43–45
   oriental 26–27

Q
quilling 18, 49, 63

R
ranunculus, spiral 10–12
recycling 6, 22, 78
roses
   faded 84–86
   musical 103–105

S
seed heads 87–89, 112–114
seed packets 24–25
spiral flowers 10–12
sunflower, fiery 78–81

T
thistle heads 94–97
tools/equipment 6
topiary cones 60–61
tulips, graphic 16–17

V
Valentine flower 106–109
vine, climbing 110–111
violets, dogtooth 98–99

W
waterlilies 53–55
wire 6, 65, 106, 112, 115
wreaths 90–93, 115–117